MW00424859

DYING
FOR A
SMOKE

DYING
FOR A
SMOKE

David A. Rives

Moon River Publishing
Ventura, California

Published by
Moon River Publishing
2646 Palma Drive
Ventura, CA 93003
(800) 522-7735

Printed in the United States of America.
10 9 8 7 6 5 4 3 2 1

First printing — November, 1991

ISBN 1-878143-06-9

"If nothing changes ...
Nothing changes."

Zen Bumper Sticker

Also by the Author:
Walk Yourself Thin

This Book is Dedicated to:

Malcolm Johnson
of
Fresno, California,
who asked that it be written;

and to the

Tobacco Companies of the World,
whom I'd love to see Malcolm outlive!

Table of Contents

1
"Satisfaction Guaranteed"

Universal Truth:

The easiest way to live is to give in to every impulse that cries out for attention:

- to eat every morsel of food that looks appetizing;
- to smoke every cigarette your system can handle;
- to gamble away your last penny;
- to drink until you pass out;

in other words: to be totally out of control every minute you're alive.

It's not a terribly **satisfying** way to live, this giving in to everything, but it is the easiest.

And why isn't it "satisfying?" After all, why are you eating or smoking or drinking all those things if not to "satisfy" yourself?

Well, yes, you're satisfying yourself, but only for the moment.

And what happens when that "moment" is over? Of course: you're worse off than when you started.

So, satisfying the momentary urge always leads to long-term destruction; and, unless you're a lot sicker than anyone's ever been, that can't lead to a whole lot of long-term satisfaction!

So, how **do** you get long-term satisfaction?

Obviously, by **controlling yourself** every now and then: by **not** eating everything in sight, **not** smoking till you throw up, etc.

And why is **self**-control so much more satisfying than being **out** of control? Because **nothing** is more satisfying than making your life better today than it was yesterday, and nothing can do that for you better than putting a lid on some of those infantile impulses of yours: a million hot fudge sundaes won't do it; neither will a million packs of Lucky's, a million fifths of Chivas or a million lottery tickets — no matter how "promising" those things look to be at the time you're doing them; and the minute you **stop** doing all those things, the minute your long-term satisfaction will automatically start to **build**!

Do you **have** to go after "long-term satisfaction?"

No: you can keep "living for the moment" and "dying by the hour," the way you always have.

We just wanted to let you know that there was a more **satisfying** way to live, in case you ever start to wonder why all those other people spend so much time smiling.

If you're like most addicts, the gas that keeps your engine running is: "I'm only here once, so why shouldn't I do every damn thing I please?!"

Well, I don't **know** why.

You're right: you **are** only here once, and once you're gone you won't be able to smoke another cigarette, eat another hot fudge sundae or gamble away the last of the rent money. So, if you **are** going to do any of those things, you're going to have to do them here, because, as far as anyone knows, there's no "there" anywhere to do them.

I'm just hoping you're reading this because you've finally said to yourself: "You know, I **am** only here once. I already know how easy it is to make the worst of things — by smoking and eating and gambling and drinking till I can't stand up. But I also know that that doesn't seem to be getting me anywhere — at least not in the **long** run — so maybe it **is** time to change direction a bit and see if I can't find a **better** way to live!"

If that **is** you talking, all we can say is: **have we got a program for you**!!

2
Define Yourself

The one thing you're going to have to do, if you're going to get off cigarettes and stay off cigarettes, is

Redefine your place in the world.

If you can't see yourself as anything but a smoker — if you're hopelessly in love with that image of yourself — then that's what you'll continue to be and, as it happens, who you'll continue to associate with, since no non-smoker yet born would ever choose to spend time with a smoker if he didn't have to — which will, of course, only reinforce your role as a smoker and make it that much **more** difficult to quit!

In other words: as long as you keep saying: "This is who I am. As far as I'm concerned, every time I light up, I'm doing something as worldly, as sophisticated as anyone has **ever** done — exactly like the advertising **promised** I would," then you really stand no chance of quitting for more than five, ten minutes, tops.

No: if you're going to become a non-smoker, you're going to have to **define** yourself as a non-smoker: someone who
  • never sets fire to a rolled-up plant and inhales the smoke that curls out of it;
  • finishes a meal with the **meal**, and not with a cigarette;
  • drives a car with **gasoline** as the only chemical pushing it forward;

3

• does **not** associate with smokers, if he can help it;

• does **not** believe a single word of the cigarette companies' expensive advertising.

Until you can do that, until you can **accept** yourself as a non-smoker, **see** yourself as a non-smoker, you have no chance of getting off cigarettes for good.

And if you **are** going to see yourself as a non-smoker, there are several things you must do:

The first is to convince yourself that the non-smoking life is not as bad as the cigarette companies make it out to be.

Yes: it's filled with geeks and wimps who have no idea how to properly christen an apartment, rope a steer, proclaim their female independence or conduct a conversation on anything above the level of a garden slug! So, if you do decide to quit smoking, you're going to have to find **other** ways to do all those things.

What other ways?

Don't know. Why don't you ask the billions of people who **don't** smoke how **they** do them?!

The next thing you'll have to do is convince yourself that the physical changes that come with not smoking are **also** not as bad as you've been led to believe:

• The pain you'll feel when lung passages that have been blocked for decades suddenly burst open again is never so great that you'll start reaching for your gun;

• The lightheadedness that comes from being able to breathe deeply for the first time in years is rarely so severe that you won't be able to work, drive, smile, etc.;

• The color that returns to your skin after you quit (get out your baby pictures if you want to know what color we're talking about) should be no cause for alarm, unless you were scheduled to star in a remake of *Night of the Living Dead* and you're allergic to make-up.

• Losing the feeling that Arnold Schwarzenegger's got a death grip on your heart is no problem: all you have to do is locate one of your ribs and press on it as hard as you can for 16 hours a day and you'll never know you've lost a thing!

Yes: the non-smoking life can be a minefield of horrors. However, if you can somehow accept that fact and just roll with the Claymores, the chances of your becoming a non-smoker will immediately take a turn for the better!

And if you can't?

Then the only thing we can see taking a turn for the better is the price of American Tobacco on the Big Board!

3
Dorian Gray

Of course, the reason it **is** so hard for a smoker to redefine himself as a non-smoker is that the two conditions are about a Universe apart. And, since no high-octane **astronaut** has ever figured out how to get from one end of the Universe to the other, you want to tell me how long I should hold my breath waiting for your neighborhood **smoker** to do it?

And yet, like it or not, that's the journey every smoker **must** take, if he's going to quit smoking. Which means it's the journey every stop-smoking program must **help** him take, if it's ever going to do him any good.

It is, of course, a lot easier to get where you're going if you know where you're at and where it is you want to go. Luckily, in the case of "smoker vs. non-smoker," that's a piece of cake:

Portrait of a Smoker	Portrait of a Non-Smoker
Smokers are, for the most part, heroic figures. They are:	Non-smokers are, for the most part, wimps. They are:
• people who, in pursuit of their habit, defy social convention every day of their lives, which means they are the only hope for real progress in the world, since nothing **impedes** progress more than slavish devotion to the status quo;	• people who would never go out on a limb for **anything**;

6

Portrait of a Smoker	Portrait of a Non-Smoker
• people who are independent, creative thinkers – people you'd want to spend the rest of your life talking to!	• people who don't see any value in experimentation; in trying new things just to discover **all** that life has to offer – physically, mentally, or, in the case of smoking, **both**! • Men and women who, as boys and girls, did everything their mommies told them to, with the result that they are among the least-interesting people to ever inhabit the Earth!
• people who risk danger every moment they're alive, since any of their million daily puffs could be the one that triggers the final heart attack – which gives them a courage a non-smoker could never **hope** to comprehend!	• people who, for some reason, consider their time far better spent not destroying their bodies.
• people who need to make a statement every minute they're alive – telling the world they're "something special," and they can do their special thing wherever and whenever they want to – much like the little children they consider themselves the exact opposite of;	• busybodies who are dedicated to destroying the very thing they should be nurturing: the smokers of the world, who are the only hope that world has of solving all its problems, since they're the only ones not hidebound by "convention."
• people who feel an automatic kinship with every other smoker on Earth – with each reinforcing his fellow smokers' convictions about the "rightness" of what each is doing.	• people who feel nothing special toward other non-smokers, thereby depriving themselves of a fellowship that is automatic among their hard-puffing brethren.

Feel free, of course, to pencil in anything about the two groups you think we might have missed. Why? Because the **more** you know about where you are and where you want to go, the better your chances of getting there.

Will this list make it **easier** for you to go from "A" to "B?"

"Yes," if all the "good" things about "A" start looking worse to you than the "awful" things about "B; but "no," if you actually "buy" all the "wonders" that "A" has to offer.

And will you?

Well, you have for most of your life. So, it wouldn't be surprising for you to **keep** buying them!

But then — we've been surprised before and, I am sure, will be again.

Maybe by the time you finish this book!

4
...but First: a Second Look

Of course, in spite of what you may be hearing and reading every day — even here — if you look at it in just the right light, you have to admit that

Smoking is NOT that bad a habit!

That's right! All it is, really, is a harmless little diversion from the helter-skelter of daily life; a relaxing way to spend a few moments alone or with some of your closest friends.

Will this "relaxing diversion" kill you? Of course it will. But it's not exactly going to do it overnight, and it's definitely not going to do it without giving you back a lifetime of pleasure. So how would you rather die: getting run over by a bus or enjoying cigarettes for 50 years?!

Do you have to give **up** something, to get this "enjoyment?"
Of course you do.
How **much** do you have to give up?
Not really that much!:

- Clear lungs.
    This could be a problem if you were thinking of running the marathon in the next Olympics. Were you?
- A few minutes every morning (and maybe a few at night), coughing up some vile-looking glop.

Question: With all the colds and flu and air pollution going around, how many people do you think **don't** cough up a lot of glop every day?

Question 2: With a full 24 hours in the day, just how excited should you be getting about "a few minutes in the morning?"

• A heart free of pain.

Yes: cigarettes can cause severe chest pain. But so can a lot of other things — fatty foods; over-exertion; stress; bad investments; Middle East crises; dirty air; clean air — so how much pain do you think you can realistically save by giving up smoking: "five per cent?" "ten per cent?" And is a "ten per cent savings" really worth all the hassle you'll have to go through, to get "divorced" from the love of your life?

• Sweet-smelling skin, clothes, hair, house, furniture, car, office, etc.

Only one question here: does it really matter how bad cigarettes make everything smell if those things don't smell bad to **you**? After all, who has to **live** with the smell 24 hours a day: you or the crybabies?

• Youthful-looking skin.

Yes, it's possible that the nicotine that's killing cells all over your body, by squeezing off the arteries that feed them, is doing the same thing to your skin. Only one question: we're taught in school that "skin" is mostly dead tissue anyway, so how badly could you possibly be hurting something that's already dead?

Besides, with all the other things that can lead to premature aging — insolent children; railroad strikes; acid rain; demise of the snail darter — why pick on smoking? Why not work on all those **other** things and **then** we can talk!?

• Relative freedom from all types of cancer.

This is the unfairest "knock" of all against smoking:

The fact is: cancer is a genetic thing — if your parents got it, you're likely to get it; if they didn't, you probably won't either, **no matter how much you smoke**!

Obviously, having the byproducts of smoking running wild through your body can't **help** your health any. But again: the effects of such chemicals could take decades to show up, so "where's the fire?"

So, **enough** about how bad a habit smoking is! All you're doing with that kind of talk is upsetting the millions of good folks who can't quit, and I'd like someone to show me the winner in **that** scenario!

Face it: smoking is nothing more than a harmless pastime — like playing the Lottery, or watching TV, or going to the races, or having a few beers — so why don't we stop with all these hysterical headlines—

"The Number One Cause of Preventable Death in the Known Universe!!"

— and start using our time and talent to help the good folks at the American Tobacco Institute find out what that Number One Killer **really** is!

In fact, here's a list of diseases the Tobacco Institute is looking into right now as the **real** "Number One Cause of Preventable Death in the Known Universe," since smoking obviously isn't; feel free to pour millions of your **own** research dollars into any of them as strikes your fancy:

1) cold sores
2) athlete's foot
3) scurvy
4) beri-beri
5) quite contrary
6) how does your
7) garden
8) grow?

5
Mmmm — GOOD!

Of course, in spite of the fact that smoking is not that bad a habit — no worse than most of the million and one **other** ways people choose to spend their time — there are always a few "oddballs" out there who wake up one morning and decide that they want to rid themselves of this "harmless diversion" once and for all.

And, since I, myself, went "oddball" on everyone, eight years ago, I think I can help those of you who want to join me do just that:

What a lot of people find helpful, when trying to get out of a jam, is to figure out how they got into one in the first place.

So, how did I get into smoking? Easy: I got into smoking because

I wanted to be a grown-up.

There was a lot about childhood I hated and, since I knew that smoking was something only grown-ups did, that made my job real simple:

You want to be a grown-up? Just start smoking.

So I did.

Was there anything going on around me, telling me **not** to smoke, because it might be **bad** for me? Well, you tell me:

• Both my parents smoked like chimneys; ditto for all my aunts and uncles (and I had a lot of those!)

So you want to tell me how bad something could be if "everybody" was doing it?

• And then there were those Saturday matinees at the Varsity Theater, kitty-corner to the University of Detroit (12 cents for a double bill, and we thought that was **high**!) :

How many heroes did I come to worship, inside those hallowed walls? Well, you remember Humphrey Bogart? You do? Then how about Robert Taylor and Gary Cooper and Clark Gable and John Wayne and John Hodiak and John Garfield and Gregory Peck and Edmund O'Brien and Paul Henreid and— and how much time do you have?

And how many of my heroes smoked up there on the big screen, with all us wide-eyed babies watching them?

You got it: **all of them**!

(Now, I don't know if the cigarette companies were **paying** my heroes to smoke up there, but, as a guy who later got addicted to the same things himself, I don't imagine they had to pay them **much**!)

So, was there anything telling this parent-worshipper/ hero-worshipper **not** to smoke? Ha! The only message **I** was getting was: "**What the Hell are you waiting for**?!"

Luckily, I didn't have to wait long:

One night, my cousin, Joyce, who was babysitting me, offered me a puff from her Viceroy. Even at that tender age (I couldn't have been more than 10 or 11), I tried to be as nonchalant about this first experience as I knew Bogie and Coop must have been about theirs.

And my nonchalance was working like a charm, until my cousin suggested that I'd probably get a lot more out of the exercise if I pulled the smoke **into** my mouth, rather than trying to blow it **out** the lit end!

I thanked her nonchalantly for this valuable tip and proceeded to do as she said.

And how was that first puff? "Disgusting?" "Revolting?" Did it make me vow, right then and there, to "never do it again?"

Ha! It was **wonderful**! It was **delicious**! I couldn't **wait** to do it again! (Unfortunately, my next puff **would** have to wait some, since my cousin cut me off after one, knowing my mother would probably do the same to her head, if she ever found out!)

So I was forced to cool my heels for a while.

Then, one day, at a cottage we were renting for the summer, I stumbled on a corncob pipe.

Since even **I** was bright enough to know what to do with a pipe, I took off for the corner store. To my surprise — and to the great relief of my pocketbook — I discovered that you could buy a box of pipe tobacco for as little as **nine cents** (remember: this was 1955)!

Well heck: even **I** could scrape together nine cents!

(Incidentally, the name of the tobacco was "Friends," and the "friends" they were talking about, as the box so clearly showed, were a pipe-smoking outdoorsman and his deliriously-faithful dog.

(I already knew, of course, from watching television, that this kind of heart-warming scene was S. O. P. in the tobacco industry, where they've always tried to hitch smoking up with our most favorite activities and loving relationships. I never knew **why** they kept trying to do this, but, judging from the millions of people who got "hooked" because of it, apparently **somebody** did!)

So I took my pipe, my tobacco and a pack of matches, grabbed my **own** best friend (no: not the barking kind!) and high-tailed it out to an old shed, in a field just beyond where our cottage "subdivision" ended.

I packed the pipe, lit it (after a few tries it even **stayed** lit) and took a drag off it (without inhaling, of course).

Well, it wasn't anywhere near as mild and tasty as my cousin's Viceroy — in fact, I might have been better off just stuffing the bowl with rolled-up marsh grass and **saving** myself the nine cents — but, hey: I was smoking!

Except there was nothing about the experience to make me want to repeat it.

So I didn't.

What I really wanted were cigarettes, but I hadn't sunk low enough yet to steal them out of my mother's purse or my father's shirt pocket, and I couldn't afford to buy them (hey: they were **25 cents a pack**!), so I had to bide my time with something I **could** afford: cigars!

In the mid-50's, you could buy a White Owl for a nickel, or a Hav-a-Tampa for six cents (talk about "mild" and "sweet-tasting!"), or a Wolf's Brothers Crooks (soaked in wine) for a dime. Since these not-so-princely sums were well within my junior high school budget, I quickly became a leading connoisseur of some of the world's finest cheroots!

Oh yes: every now and then a cigarette would come my way, and I would "enjoy" it (though, again, never inhaling it). But, for stupendous flavor and real sit-back-and-relax pleasure, you couldn't beat a cigar (**still** can't, of course, but, since there's no way I can trust myself not to inhale, I've forgotten they even exist)!

Eventually, of course, I **did** figure out a way to steal my mother's smokes (since she usually kept an open pack of Kents in her dresser drawer, it wasn't all **that** difficult!) and eventually I **did** start to inhale (more about that later), which is how I eventually **did** "buy" myself a cigarette habit, (and, I would imagine, is real similar to the way you eventually "bought" yours!)

And how did I manage to finally "un-buy" it, a third-of-a-century later? Through a set of lucky circumstances:

It all started when a 400-pound friend of mine found out you could make extra money, umpiring softball games. Since they had openings for more than one umpire, he asked if I'd like to join him.

Well, when we first met, I, myself, was tipping the scales at a cool 250 and could move only slightly faster than a rock. So, if he had asked me about umpiring then, I would have said "Yes."

However, by the time the job **did** become available, I had slimmed down to about 170 and was having "no problem" slipping into Size 31 slacks; so I was looking more like a ball **player** than a ball **umpire**.

Which is why, when he asked me about umpiring, I turned the tables on him and asked him if he knew how I might go about joining a team and **playing** instead.

He did.

At the first practice with my new team, I came up to bat and tagged one — far over the right fielder's head, with that one in hot, though apparently futile, pursuit.

I knew when I hit it that it was most likely a home run — especially since there weren't any fences — but I wasn't taking any chances: I **bolted** out of the batter's box, on a beeline for first base.

Well, two steps out of the box the thigh muscles in my legs turned to stone and decided they had **better** ways to spend the afternoon than getting me to first base — or any **other** base that came to mind!

Which is how I managed to turn what should have been a "double home run" into a "close play at third!"

When it came time for us to take the field, I called to the player next to me and told him to "cover" for me if any balls came our way, since I was now in **Michaelangelo's** "ballpark!"

I finished up the practice (don't ask me how) and knew that, if I didn't get myself into the **shape** of a ballplayer pretty quick, it wouldn't matter how much I **looked** like one!

It just so happened that, right about that time, another friend of mine had gotten into running, to take off some of his excess desserts. Since my legs had been "done in" by running, I figured it would take running to get them right again. So I invited myself to join him on his daily jaunts.

Since I was smoking two packs a day at the time (and if you ever saw me you'd swear it was closer to **four**!), I was "all out" to finish a mile, and to run it in anything under 12 minutes; after which, I'd cough my guts out for another 12 minutes, until my lungs were clear enough to run a second mile or to light up my first post-run cigarette!

This went on for about three weeks: my legs getting better and better and my smoking doing just fine, thank you.

By the end of those three weeks, I'd managed to whittle my mile time down to around 10 minutes — or about 10 seconds a day better than when I'd started.

At which point, another friend, who'd stopped smoking some nine months before, using the Seventh-Day Adventist Program, collared me and told me that the program was starting up again the following Monday and would I be interested in attending?

Since my new running program had shown me, in no uncertain terms, the toll my nearly-lifelong smoking habit had been taking on my lungs, I told him "Yes," and he enrolled me right there on the spot.

The program started in the church's chapel, the night of September 12, 1983.

What's that?: "Did I really want to give up smoking?"

Well, you tell me:

As we were driving over for the first session, I asked my friend if they let you smoke during the meetings.

"Well," he answered, "they're being held in a chapel......."

He didn't have to finish the sentence. I knew the **last** thing anybody'd be doing was "smoking in a chapel!"

"Damn!" I thought. "Not letting you smoke during a 'stop-smoking' course?! I mean, what could be more stressful to a smoker than the thought of never smoking again?! And how am I going to relieve that stress if I can't light up?!

"And these people call themselves 'emissaries of God?!' Give me a break!" I grumbled, and scowled my way to the nearest pew!

Does that kind of answer your question about how ready I was to quit?!

And yet, quit I did, to the utter amazement of anyone who'd ever seen me smoke — especially the guys I played bridge with (**"Rives quit**?! The **'Human Chimney' QUIT**?!")

And how did I do it? What was it that tipped the scales on the side of never smoking again?

Just this:

Eighteen hours after that first stop-smoking class, I hopped out for my afternoon run. (And remember: in the three weeks since I'd **been** running, the best mile I'd ever done was 10 minutes, and I got there by slicing around ten seconds a day off my "personal best.")

So, how fast did I run a mile, that first day of not smoking? Would you believe: "**9:30**!"

That's right: by staying off the smokes for just 18 hours I was able to chop a **full 30 seconds** off my best mile time till then!

Of course, I still couldn't go much beyond a mile before "dying," but who cared?: "**Thirty seconds!!**"

The next day — my second without cigarettes — when I got to the end of the first mile, I **wasn't** "dying." So, I went on to do a second mile. Then a third!

And then I checked my time for those three miles: under 30 minutes!

Wow!: a better time, for each of **three** miles, than I'd recorded for just a **single** mile, only two days before!

Was I "sold" on not smoking?

Could Richard Nixon steal??

Will this work for you the way it worked for me: using an exercise program to make you see just how much of your physical ability you've lost to cigarettes? And will finding out how much you've lost be enough to make you want to get it back?

I don't know.

One thing I do know, though: if you **don't** give yourself a chance to see what smoking has cost you, you'll **never** have a reason to quit, because as long as you don't move very much, you'll forever think you "haven't lost a step," so "what's the problem??"

So do it. Get out there and just start walking (forget about "running" for a while) — as far and as fast as your legs (and lungs) will carry you.

Challenge those lungs; **make** them work! Only then will you see how little of their capacity you have left, how much of their power you've lost.

Again: will this be enough to get you to turn your back on cigarettes forever?

I don't know. And neither will you — till you try.

So, do it!

Now!

6
"...line and sinker!"

The best thing about cigarettes, of course, is that you can't get "hooked" on them, like you can on heroin or cocaine or booze.

You were probably brought up with this "fact" (you can't remember who told it to you, but obviously **someone** did), and it was one of the main reasons you had no fear about taking up the habit at the age of 14 or15, since you knew you could always get rid of it by the time you were **16**, so what's the big deal?

Of course, after you began smoking, some people started telling you differently — older people, people who had already been smoking for a while. They said you **can** get hooked, that you **can't** just give it up whenever you want to!

But what did they know? They were they and you were you, and even though you felt sorry for them for not having a clue about what you could and could not control, was that any reason to let them tell you how to run your life?!

After all, how hard could it be to stop puffing away on a **weed**, for God's sake?! I mean, it's a stupid thing to do from the get-go — breathing in smoke from a burning plant — so how hard could it be to **stop** doing something that dumb?! Give me a break!

So, you did start; and you found that you **were** able to control it:

As long as you weren't inhaling, you could smoke one cigarette or a hundred on Monday and never desire another one on Tuesday or the rest of your life.

"See? Told you it was 'no sweat!'"

And then someone suggested that you take the smoke into your lungs — that you'd get more "enjoyment" that way.

And so you did — usually in the privacy of your own room, since this promised to be something "special" and that's where you first did **all** your special things!

And, when you'd finished your first inhaled cigarette, you sat there or lay there, basking in the glorious sensation of nicotine numbing your brain and making the whole world seem a lot more pleasant place to live than it had only a few minutes before.

And the sensation was so strong that it carried you along for hours, without any need for "reinforcement."

Until the next day, when you again flew to your room after school to repeat that most wonderful "high."

And day after day that one cigarette was all it took.

Until, one day, it wasn't. Or until one day you decided that if that cigarette made your **after**-school time so enjoyable, why not make your **during**-school time just as enjoyable by having a smoke in the morning?

And then: one during recess?

And then: one on the way home?

Do we have to fill in the rest of that first smoking year for you or have you already done it for us?

Let's just say that, unless you were someone the Pope had been looking high and low for, by the end of that year you were signing your name to a "contract" from Philip Morris or R. J. Reynolds or the American Tobacco Company, agreeing to devote your every waking moment to consuming their wonderful products.

And why shouldn't you? You were doing something enjoyable weren't you, and how many of those type things are there around that you can just turn your back on even a single one of them?!

So you **didn't** turn your back on it. You **embraced** it. It was "you" now, and, you had to admit, you didn't really **mind** the identification, since it set you apart from the rest of the crowd (read: "non-smoking wimps!")

Which, of course, is how you very quickly got hooked on something that you "knew" could **never** hook you!

We've often wondered what would have happened if, rather than using the word "smoking" for what you do with a cigarette — which conjures up all sorts of comfortable, "homey" images — people had used the phrase "taking a drug" instead. Would it have made any difference?

Probably not — at least not to the majority of people who take up the habit. The blissful sedation and the instant-macho identification that come from lighting up are such powerful cues to **continue** lighting up that the average new smoker could care less **what** you called his wonderful habit, as long as you kept him in smokes!

The only reason we even **ask** the question is because we keep seeing this hopelessly-naive little 12-year-old in our minds, about to inhale for the first time, and being warned that he's not about to "start smoking;" that what he's **really** about to start doing is "taking a drug!"

And, in this pipedream of ours, the little boy answers: "You mean, like 'heroin?' Or 'cocaine?'"

"That's right."

"No thanks!"

And he puts the match out, hands us the cigarette and walks away from smoking forever!

We want the dream to come true, of course, because that little boy is us, and, if nothing else, we'd like to get back the 23 years-worth of money we threw away on cigarettes (luckily, we needn't dream of getting our health back, since that appears to have come back all by itself, thanks to a body that seems to get some kind of "kick" out of renewing itself, once you stop "insulting" it [as the doctors say] with a nonstop barrage of red-hot nicotine and tar).

Of course, even if someone **did** call it a "drug" when everyone else was calling it "smoking," who among us wouldn't have answered: "Well, how bad a drug could it be if **everybody's** 'taking' it?! I mean, these people can't **all** be stupid! They're grown-ups, for Pete's sake, and grown-ups **always** know what they're doing!

"So, if they're smoking, they must know it can't hurt them. So how could it hurt me?!"

It wasn't until later, as we watched our heroes — the Bogarts, Taylors, Coopers and Gables of the world — vanish, one after another, each in his own puff of smoke, that we started thinking: "Hey: maybe this habit isn't so 'chummy' after all. Maybe it's a 'killer,' no matter how 'enjoyable' it is!"

By then, of course, it was too late: we were hooked. And since we were, what good would it do to frighten ourselves by dwelling on the "downside" of smoking?

So we didn't.

Instead, we watched the TV, and then the magazine ads, to see how other people were enjoying the habit we all loved so much.

And as they laughed, so did we; as they came "Alive with pleasure," so did we. And the grim statistics about smoking became, in a flash, the exclusive property of "the other guy."

Hopefully, those of us who have been lucky enough to quit will never become "the other guy." But, if we do wake up one day with lung cancer or bladder cancer or emphysema, I hope we'll at least have wised up enough by that time to have seen through the slick ads — the ones that seem to be saying: "Hey: don't blame us; all we're promoting is a harmless, fun activity" — and can finally "point the finger" where it should be pointed: at the cigarette companies, where the only people **truly** alive with pleasure are the ones behind the cash register!

7

"...and then came the pole!"

In the last chapter, we mentioned that we all got into smoking because we "knew" it wasn't physically-addicting, like "hard" drugs were, so we could quit it anytime we wanted to, and without going through all the withdrawal miseries we'd seen in *Lost Weekend, Man with a Golden Arm, Panic in Needle Park*, etc.

"Of course," we asked ourselves, "why would anyone want to quit something that was so (cough) enjoyable?"

So, we **didn't** quit. We kept right on smoking. Year after year.

Until, one day, we did decide to quit. And found out, as we went through our **own** *Lost Weekend*, just how "non-physically-addicting" cigarettes really were!

So that barrier to quitting, which we thought didn't exist, was in fact very real.

In all honesty, though, as strong a barrier as it is to overcome, physical addiction to cigarettes still can't hold a candle to its "better half:" psychological addiction!

And why is the psychological addiction so much stronger?

Because the chemical addiction is the result of just one thing: a sedative with predictable effects when you "take" it and predictable effects when you take it away!

But smoking is far more than just a **chemical** habit:

23

The problem with smoking is that it becomes a part of everything we do:
- getting up in the morning;
- shaving;
- making a phone call;
- starting the car;
- talking to someone;
- following a meal;
- before and/or after sex (also "during," for **some** of you Marlboro Men!);
- etc.

In fact, because we've been smoking along with all those activities for so long, our brains now think we **have** to smoke to do those things, and you wind up with the pathetic sight of people who absolutely **can't** make a phone call or start their car without lighting up first!

And please understand: this has nothing to do with the need for the **chemicals** in cigarettes. The average smoker's bloodstream is **saturated** with those chemicals after his first cigarette of the day. So whatever "need" he feels for a cigarette after that is all "psychological."

And why is this psychological need so much harder to conquer than the chemical need?

Because, as we just said: the chemical need deals with only one thing — "sedation" — whereas the psychological need may be an intimate part of a **hundred** different things! And I don't know about you, but the thought of changing a hundred different activities all at once does not give me a nice, warm glow in the pit of my stomach — unless you consider the high point of "swallowing hot coals" to be the "nice, warm glow" it gives you!

So let's not trivialize the psychological addictiveness of cigarettes by thinking of it as something that **anybody** should be able to conquer. The fact is: it's about as "trivial" a thing to conquer as Everest!

Is it **impossible** to conquer?
Is Everest?

The fact is: the psychological addictiveness of smoking can be overcome fairly easily. All you have to do is remember one thing:

There was a time in your life when you DIDN'T need to smoke a cigarette to do all of those things, and yet you managed to do them all quite well.

So, even though a cigarette now **accompanies** all those activities, it's not really **necessary** for the activity, no matter how much it **feels** like it is — a fact which is, of course, borne out by the millions of people your age who shave, shower, eat, drive, talk, work, etc., and not only **don't** need a cigarette to do all those things, but have **never** needed one!

All you have to do, then, is go back, in your mind, to a time when you lived without cigarettes, a time before you took that fatal first step — which, since you're reading this, we assume you now want to "**un**take"— and merely **untake it**!:

Picture yourself getting out of bed as a youngster and **not** lighting up as your feet hit the floor;

See yourself going to school **without** a cigarette dangling "coolly" from your lips;

Tell yourself that there's **nothing** "macho" in flooding your lungs with searing smoke, that it was something you let yourself get talked into before you were smart enough to know any better!

In other words: we're not asking you to break any new ground here — a frightening prospect no matter **what** you're trying to do. All we're asking is that you go back mentally to the time **before** you started smoking and pretend you never started; to keep living as you once lived: free of cigarettes and not missing them for a minute!

You know, the most wonderful thing about our brains is that they will take us wherever we tell them we want to go. Advertisers know this, which is why **they** tell our brains where we want to go before **we** have a chance to!

No problem there — we all "advertise" **something** — as long as we can use that knowledge to our own advantage. And, by picturing a life we want to live — a life free of cigarettes — we will be giving our brains the best cue they could get, and the only one they really need, to take us there.

So, do it! Picture a meal ending with the meal, not with a cigarette; picture driving your car with the ashtray shut and with your hands and mouth free of any "encumbrances;" picture a round of golf where the only things you light up are the red numbers on the scoreboard!

And, when it comes time to **do** all those things — finish that meal, drive that car, play that round of golf — here's a way to "help" your picture come true:

At the point where you would normally light up, take as deep a breath as you can instead — and keep taking deep breaths until the urge to smoke leaves you, or until you feel too light-headed to continue!

What will this do?

It will simply remind you of what you will be giving up if you do light up.

Will this work the first time you try it? Yes, for a few of you; no, for most.

Will it work eventually?

Well, if it doesn't — if the feeling of clear lungs isn't enough to make want you to **keep** them clear — I really don't know what else will!

Believe me: it works!
And how can you tell?
Just try it and see!

A few more thoughts about physical addiction versus psychological addiction:

The reason people believed that cigarettes were not physically addicting, back in the 40's and 50's (aside from the obvious fact that cigarette companies didn't **want** anybody thinking he could get hooked on their product, which would have been bad for business, so they spent a lot of money **telling** you you couldn't) was because, unlike the two **major** physical addictors — heroin and booze — the drug in cigarettes does **not** enter cells in the body and replace a chemical in one of those cells' normal reactions. So, withdrawing from that drug — nicotine — should be a lot easier, on paper at least, than withdrawing from either heroin or alcohol.

And, as we said earlier: it was just such "knowledge" that gave us the confidence to take the cigarette plunge, since we knew we could always get out of the "pool" any time we wanted to. Until, one day, we tried — and found out we couldn't!

Of course, we now know that cigarettes are **very** physically addicting, that drugs don't have to replace chemicals in a cell's **deepest** reactions, the way heroin and alcohol do, as long as they take the place of some chemicals somewhere, thereby making the body "hunger" for those chemicals when they're suddenly taken away.

The problem with this new knowledge, of course, is that it has given a whole generation of smokers a new lease on their smoking lives: instead of expecting themselves to quit at the drop of a hat, as we all thought we could, 30 or 40 years ago, these smokers can now throw up their hands and say: "Why look at me?! Get all those boozers and junkies to quit and **then** we can talk!"

And when the boozers and junkies **don't** quit? Of course: the smokers don't either. And why should we expect them to, since we now know that theirs is as "deep" a physical dependence as any drunk or junkie ever knew?

Well, fine — cigarettes are physically addicting and that is important. But the fact is: what we were told/taught in the 40's and 50's was **not** all wrong; after all, it wasn't **only** cigarette company shills who were touting the non-addictive nature of smoking (at least I don't think it was).

The plain truth is: Yes, cigarettes are physically addicting — but that only represents about 10% of their addictive power.

What accounts for the other 90%?

Of course: The very thing that everyone was talking about 50 years ago: its psychological addictiveness!

And why are cigarettes psychologically addicting?

Well, why is there a need for drugs at all?

Obviously: because the world is a mighty stressful place to live and drugs make it seem a lot less so. So, who **wouldn't** grab at something that can relieve so much agony so quickly and easily?

Which is why, for example, you originally lit up before starting your car: the thought that within minutes you'd be jousting for road space with a bunch of lunatics who **may** learn how to drive before they die but you doubt it, was so stressful that you really had no choice **but** to light up.

Which is the reason you've lit up before starting your car ever since .

Except...

Go out into the country, where the nearest soul is a hundred miles away, where the word "stress" isn't even in the dictionary, and watch what you do before starting your car! Mm-hm.

So whatever the **original** reason for lighting up, that's been buried as long as Caesar. Now you light up because you've **"always"** lit up and you don't feel comfortable **not** lighting up!

Why don't you?

Because lighting up before you start your car has become a habit — just as it has when you first wake up, take a shower, brush your teeth, eat breakfast, wash the dog and *ad nauseum* .

And why has it become a habit?

Because your Subconscious Mind has made it so (we call it the "**Sub**conscious Mind" because it makes us do everything we do, but without ever telling us **why**!)

And why does your Subconscious Mind make smoking a habit?

Because your Subconscious Mind has only one function: to make sure you survive, since, if you die, it dies, and it can't let that happen.

And how can something as deadly as "smoking" possibly have "survival value?"

Easy:

Every day you do two things:

1) You smoke cigarettes;

2) You live to see tomorrow.

Unfortunately, your Subconscious Mind makes the fatal mistake of **connecting** those two things, imagining that your smoking was the **reason** you survived — not that hard a mistake to make since you did do both, so why **wouldn't** they be connected? And, since your survival is all your Subconscious cares about, that would seem to make its job rather easy: since it looks like all it took was a pile of cigarettes to get you from yesterday to today, what better way to get you to tomorrow than to dump the same pile of cigarettes on you all over again?! Which it does!

How?

By driving you crazy if you **don't** smoke them: making you a nervous wreck until you're once again satisfying its **psychological** needs by filling your body with smoke!

That's right: it's your **Subconscious** that makes you reach into pocket or purse every five minutes for a smoke; it's nothing that **you** are doing **consciously**!

And that's where the trouble starts:

Once you start doing something "automatically" — doing it out of subconscious habit — it becomes so **easy** to do that you forget there could be bad consequences attached to it: after all, how bad could something be if it's as easy to do as shaving your face, using a knife and fork, etc.?

How to get around this? How to stop doing something that you're not really **conscious** of doing?

Easy: **Become** conscious of doing it!

That's right: Go back to the beginning, when you had to make a conscious effort to do everything related to smoking, and make it conscious once again:

taking the cigarette out of the pack with just the right flick of the wrist;

grabbing it from the pack with your lips at a point exactly 20 millimeters from the corner of your mouth;

lighting the match the way Bogie and Coop used to;

then lighting the cigarette and taking that first drag in a way that would have movie directors standing in line for your autograph, if they just knew where to find you!

Thought you were pretty cool, didn't you — learning all that stuff in front of a mirror when you were 12 or 15?

Well, you're **not** 12 or 15 any more. But you can still find your way to a mirror. So that's where we want you to go.

Why?

To start all over again: to imagine you're learning to be "cool" all over again, copying all the smoking adults you admired back then, adults now dead of the "coolness" you'll be so carefully relearning.

Still impressed with yourself, the way you were back then?

Well, keep looking at yourself — at how childish you look — until you're **not** impressed!

And when you get up in the morning and reach for that first smoke? Be **conscious** of what you're doing: **conscious** that you're about to set fire to a weed and inhale the smoke that results from it; **conscious** that you're about to subject the only heart and lungs you'll ever have (forget transplants!) to the **last** thing they could possibly want: searing heat and noxious chemicals!

Will this work the first time you try it? No: you'll probably light up anyway. But **keep at it**! You'll never kick the habit if you let it stay **un**conscious, so **be conscious** of what you're doing, every time you do it!

And what can happen when you become conscious of what you're doing to yourself? Of course: there's a chance you'll **stop** doing it to yourself.

And what will that do?

Well, in the same way you tell your Subconscious that you want to smoke by **smoking**, you'll be telling it you **don't** want to smoke by **not** smoking!

Again: your Subconscious will try to get you to do everything on Tuesday that you did on Monday. So, if you smoke all day Monday, it will try to get you to smoke all day Tuesday, thinking that's what you **need** to do, to survive. But, if you **don't** smoke on Monday, it will **have no reason** to make you smoke on Tuesday; until, after a few days of this, your Subconscious will imbue "**not** smoking" with as much survival value as "smoking" used to have! At which point, it will become as hard to **smoke** as it used to be **not** to smoke (not really: you'll still have the "drug thing" to contend with, but that's a piece of cake compared to the "habit thing!")

And all it will take is a few days of **not** smoking to show your Subconscious exactly what you want it to do.

So give it those few days! After all: you've given cigarettes a few **decades**, so it's not exactly like we're demanding "equal time" here!

And if, after those few days of trying to change your **smoking** habit into an equally-powerful **not-smoking** habit, you decide you'd rather not? No problem: just start back up again! No one will stop you; the cigarette companies will still be in business; you can always hit someone up for a light (though you may have trouble finding a place that will let you smoke the thing once you do have it lit, but that's between you and the [enlightened] management!)

All we're asking is that you at least **try** to use the knowledge of why you crave cigarettes so desperately — a misguided Subconscious that thinks you "need" cigarettes, to survive — to give yourself a chance to **not** crave them so desperately, which you do by taking a few days off them to "reprogram" that Subconscious.

So try to do that.

And if it doesn't succeed the first time?

No problem: try again. After all: how many things in your life have you done exactly right the first time through (if your answer was on the plus side of "none," you've been smoking a lot more than just cigarettes!)?

Again: all we're saying is, you now have knowledge that you probably didn't have before. And unless you're living in a different universe than we are, "knowledge" is and always will be "power," and "power" is exactly what it's going to take to kick a habit you should never have gotten into in the first place!

So, **use** the power you've gained, to rid yourself of something you're better off without!

Will you regret going off cigarettes?

If you do, you'll be the first.

Will you go back on them anyway, sometime in the future?

If you do, you won't be the last!

Why is this?

Because it's easier to bury our heads in the sand and pretend that we can get the sedation we "need" without paying a "price" — even though nothing **else** we've done has ever been "free!" — than to face up to what we're **really** doing with our lives!

So, while you're being "conscious" of smoking to **get** yourself off the habit, be "conscious" as well of just how bad your life was **while** you were smoking, so you can **keep** yourself off the habit.

And one other thing to be conscious of: the incredible number of people who **don't** have to light up every five minutes — or every five **decades** — to live perfectly-wonderful lives! You think **all** of them are wimps, all of them "losers," who don't know the pleasure they're missing?

Or might you find the real "loser" somewhere else — maybe in that mirror we just sent you to; you know: the one where Bogie and Coop and Bette are standing behind you, urging you on to more "coolness" and more "sophistication" than even Philip Morris would have dreamt possible!

Or dreamt you needed.

8
Not so Trivial

Certain people would like you to believe that smoking is just a small part of your life, that it's nothing more than a pleasant addition to everything else you do during the day.

Right: and an asteroid, crashing into the Earth at a hundred miles a second, would represent just a "pleasant little addition" to our planet!

No way: Smoking isn't a "small part of your life;" smoking **is** your life; everything else is just a sideshow!:

Driving a car is nothing special; it's the cigarette you have **while** you're driving that's special! Breakfast is just a meal; it's the cigarette you have **after** that breakfast that **really** counts! And on and on throughout the day.

Smoking makes up what psychologists call your **identity**: the way you think of yourself, the way you'd like the **world** to think of you. In other words:

Smoking IS You;
You are Smoking.

Which means that "giving up smoking" is the same as "giving up your life," which has to be a no-no in almost **anybody's** book — and which is why most smokers would rather **die** than give up their one true love — and do so with depressing regularity.

Anyway, there's the source of the problem: every time you light up, you're not just setting fire to a dead plant; you're announcing to the world: "This is me! This is who I am! This is the way I like to see myself!" — the same way **anybody** who's doing what he wants to do likes to "see" himself: doctor, lawyer, salesman, housewife, ax-murderer, etc.

If you're a smoker, what you're saying is: "I **like** seeing myself as a smoker: suave, cool, sophisticated; as different from your unsophisticated, non-smoking wimp as I can possibly be!

"I **love** the way I light my cigarette, hold my cigarette, inhale my cigarette, flick my ashes, get sedated, finish off a meal, chat with other smokers, etc.

"And it doesn't matter how many times you call me a 'pathetic loser' for my habit, because I just don't see myself that way. In fact, quite the opposite, since, every time I light up, I see myself as **winning out** over the boredom of not having anything else in my life as exciting, as different, as smoking.

"I see myself beating back the forces of nervousness and anxiety that can **ruin** a life, by giving myself what I consider no more than a mild sedative.

"And, quite frankly, if you weren't so biased and tried seeing things from **my** perspective for a change, I can't help but believe that you'd **stop** calling me a 'loser' and start seeing me for the winner I so obviously am!"

Right: you hold your breath......

O.K., so cigarettes are your "identity" and that "identity" is making you a "winner!" That's nice. So, where does it say that any one of a thousand **other** identities wouldn't make you just as big a "winner" — and without your having to give up so much in terms of health, etc., to be one?!

So, yes: you have an identity; and it's **your** identity, so you're in love with it, you're comfortable with it. It is "you" and you have no reason to give it up. Fine!

All we're saying is: it's just a **fluke** that something like "smoking" came to be "you" in the first place; **anything** could have come along, at the point in your life when you were searching for an identity, and been just as "you" as smoking so easily became.

And, since it could have been anything at the time you were **choosing** your identity — a time when, for some reason, all the cigarette companies try to outdo one another in making sure you never run short of free smokes — it could be anything **now**!

In other words: Just because it's your identity, just because it's "you," where does it say it has to **stay** "you?!" If it was just a fluke — albeit a well-**engineered** fluke — that you became a smoker in the first place, what's to say you couldn't engineer your **own** fluke at this stage of the game and start becoming a **different** "you?!"

What sort of "different 'you?'"

Well, how about a "**non**-smoker," for starters?

That's right: where does it say you can't take the same pride in your ability **not** to have a hundred cigarettes a day as you now take in lighting **up** whenever and wherever you please?!

Is it easy to change identities?

No: the one you've got has a 20- or 30-year head start on the one you're trying to get and even Secretariat might have had trouble overcoming that kind of lead.

Is it **impossible** to overcome?

No: all it takes is time (you remember: the stuff that "heals all wounds?") — time...and a target, because I don't care how much time you give to something, if you have no clear idea of where you're going, you want to guess how much time it'll take to get there?!

And what sort of "target" are we talking about?

Of course: The life you **should** be living, **would have been living**, if it weren't for the tidal wave of "public opinion" way back when — the wave that convinced you that smoking was the most wonderful way a 12-year-old could spend eternity!

And how do you go about setting up this "target?"

Well, the easiest way to quit smoking is to simply visualize what your life would be like as a non-smoker and then just "put" yourself **into** that life.

In Chapter 7, we advised doing it by going **back** in time, to a point where cigarettes were the **furthest** thing from your mind and yet you seemed to manage quite well, thank you.

There is, of course, no reason not to try doing it by going **forward** in time, to a "place" where you will, in fact, be exactly like any **other** non-smoker. To wit:

1) A smoker can't wait to light up in the morning — doing so, in some cases, even before he's rolled over in bed (especially if he spent the night before with John Barleycorn);

A non-smoker, on the other hand, thinks of tons of things between the time he's first conscious in the morning and the time he jumps out of bed, but "setting fire to a weed and inhaling noxious vapors" is never one of them!

Your task? Copy the non-smoker: **Do** tons of things, **think** of tons of things when you first wake up: your spouse, your job, your family (yes, they all have their faults — who doesn't? — but those faults aren't going to get any **better** with you forever lost in a cloud of smoke!) Just **don't** think of lighting a cigarette — in exactly the same way billions of **other** non-smokers don't think of lighting one!

What you might do instead, for the first few days, is to grab your Cig Sub, or a piece of candy, or your baby's pacifier, so you'll have **something** in your mouth that'll fool your Subconscious Mind — just not something that's sent out from North Carolina every day with instructions to kill you!

2) A smoker has to schedule his morning shower around coughing jags;

A non-smoker can step into the shower anytime he pleases — and so will you, after your lungs have reversed the 10 or 20 years of abuse you've treated them to (might take as long as a couple, three **months** to undo those decades of damage!).

3) A smoker can't wait to **finish** his shower, so he can light up again, the instant the water is off (a few pathetic puffers have even tried to rig up something that will let them smoke **inside** the shower: a tube-like device, with the cigarette stuck in one end, outside the shower, and the "business end" of the tube draped over the inside of the shower door. Luckily, I was never one of the poor unfortunates haunted by such grotesque visions — though, if I had been, No. 10 clear brake line would probably have done the trick!)

A non-smoker, in contrast, **luxuriates** in the shower, and the only **post**-shower thoughts he has deal mainly with finishing up the rest of his morning routine — shave, hair, teeth, etc. — but without fighting through a cloud of industrial waste to do it!

Your task? Once again: picture yourself doing any of the million things that non-smokers do in the morning. Just don't picture yourself doing the one in a million they don't — the one in a million that, as it happens, will most likely find them still showering long after you've been "planted!"

4) A smoker eats breakfast with only one thought in mind: the cigarette he'll be lighting up before the last morsel of food has even cleared his palate (in fact, some smokers go so far as to make sure their handsomely-shaped, tastefully-decorated packs of cigarettes are right out there where they can see them — on table or counter top — so they can be constantly reminded of the joy that will be theirs when the meal is done (yes, Virginia, drugs are a "joy" — only a fool would pretend they're not — and your good buddies, Philip and R. J., are definitely no fools!);

A non-smoker, on the other hand, eats his breakfast (or lunch or dinner) with only one thought in mind: finishing up as quickly as possible, so he can return to the excitement of his personal or business life as quickly as possible — without devoting **half** of that life chained to a food trough, "relaxing" with a cigarette (I mean, how much "relaxation" do you need, when your life is already full of autofocus cameras; remote controls for your TV, VCR, stereo, etc.; cars that tell **you** when their oil needs changing; washing machines that probably have a cycle for your neighbor's Beechcraft, if you could just figure it out; and on and on?)

Your task, to become a non-smoker? Of course: **don't** look forward to a cigarette after every meal! Don't look forward to **anything**, except the positive things that every non-smoker looks forward to (if you do need something to look forward to, look forward to a piece of hard candy, or your Cig Sub, or playing catch with your kids for a while [or with your boss, if that's what he's into]. Just don't look forward to something you'd never have **started** looking forward to, if someone hadn't talked you into it!)

5) A smoker can't start his car or make a phone call without lighting up first;

For some reason, a non-smoker's car and phone seem to work quite nicely, thank you, without a steady stream of nicotine and tar running through them!

The solution?: Either trade in your car and phone or do something **else** before you start them. **What** else? **Anything** else!

We could go on with this forever, but you get the point: as long as **one** person doesn't have to light up before, during or after everything he does in life, why do you? What's so special about him (or you) that you "absolutely can't do without" something he has trouble seeing any use for in the first place?!

The answer?: the only thing "special" about him is that he never got roped in by the con job that cigarette companies are masters at — the same con job that most likely sucked your parents in: "Smokers are sophisticated, worldly, 'alive,' creative, etc., etc." — which in turn gave you the greenest light you could ever want for your **own** descent into "Nicotine Nirvana!"

And how do you pull yourself **out** of that heavenly trap?

Easy: you just "**un**-con" yourself.

That's right: You step back and look at what you're **really** doing to yourself, every time you light up: giving your entire existence over to a drug, which isn't making you sophisticated or worldly or creative or anything else but sicker and sicker, then dead.

And why do you keep making this daily "donation?"

Because you "**enjoy**" smoking!

Well fine. But then answer me this: How come every single **non**-smoker seems to be getting a heck of a lot more joy out of life than you could ever **dream** of?! Huh?

You think all those people jogging around your neighborhood — or biking or Thinwalking or rollerblading — are doing it because they **don't** enjoy it?! You think the feeling of being able to fill every last inch of your lungs with life-giving, exercise-facilitating air is **not** enjoyable?! Come off it!

Yeah, you "enjoy" smoking. But don't you think you owe it to yourself to see if there might not be a **higher** level of joy you could attain, if you could just put smoking's **gutter** level of "joy" behind you?

And if you're **not** happier not smoking?

No problem: just start up again! After all: millions of weaklings have and millions more will, so you'll never be alone!

All we're saying is: At least give yourself a **chance** to experience what non-smokers take for granted, every minute they're alive: a life free of terminal lung congestion, terminal coughing, terminal drug addiction; terminal weakness; terminal canc—...oops, sorry, can't say that: it's never been "proven" (and if you buy that, I've got a great deal on some vacation land just outside Boca Raton.......)

And how do you free yourself of all of smoking's terminal "joys?" Easy: by imagining you're **already** a non-smoker and then just slipping yourself into that new lifestyle, in the same way you'd slip yourself into a new pair of slacks.

Will such a technique allow you to go from smoker to non-smoker overnight? It should — especially if you can keep your mouth occupied with any number of pacifiers while you're making the transition.

And if those pacifiers don't work? Well then you might try doing what every non-smoker does without thinking: Breathing as deeply as God intended you to — as often as your little heart desires.

Why? For just one reason:

BECAUSE YOU CAN!

9
Decisions, Decisions!

Of course, before you quit smoking, you'd better make sure it's the right thing to do.

The best way to do that, of course, is to weigh the pros and cons of such a move.

First, the "cons:"

1) The minute you quit smoking, you threaten the livelihood of thousands of "line workers" at P. Lorillard, R. J. Reynolds, The American Tobacco, etc. If you can't stand the thought of putting so many nice folks out of work, you'd better think twice about quitting.

Of course, you **could** console yourself with the fact that your quitting won't be putting any tobacco company **executives** out of work — somehow they **always** manage to survive — so you won't be committing **that** much economic terrorism throughout the mid-South, though you will be committing **some** and you should be aware of it — at least as aware as the tobacco companies are of theirs!

2) The minute you quit, the overall value of companies like RJR/Nabisco (parent of such brands as Camel, Winston, Salem, etc.) will start to go down, which will make the hopelessly-leveraged buyout of such a company, recently engineered by the egos of Kohlberg, Kravis and Roberts, look like an even

worse deal than it was to begin with — which will make those three gentlemen look a lot less genius-like than they actually are!

So, if the thought of singlehandedly destroying the psyches of three zillionaires from the Big Apple will keep you tossing and turning all night, then you should reverse your decision immediately and run out and buy a five-cent pack of Camels (What's that: a pack **doesn't** cost "five cents?" Funny: that's what it costs to **make**! How much more could it cost to **buy**? WHAT?! THAT MUCH?! Get my broker on the phone — NOW!!)

3) The minute you quit, you threaten a weed, growing down in North Carolina, with the prospect of "dying on the vine" — a cruel fate for **any** plant, and no **less** so for one called "tobacco."

Luckily, you won't be threatening the livelihood of the farmer who **grows** that tobacco, since he gets paid whether he harvests the stuff or not (something called "government subsidies;" you remember: what **schools** used to get!)

So, if you can't stand the thought of that weed dying without ever getting its once-in-a-lifetime opportunity to take you down with it, then for God's sake: KEEP SMOKING!

4) The minute you quit, all the people who've been telling you you "can't smoke here" and you "can't smoke there" will stop telling you **anything** — except, maybe, how nice your cologne smells.

If you don't think you'll be able to stand this sudden lack of attention — if you **like** picketing for "Smokers' Rights" (the primary one being the right to kill everyone around you with your habit!) — then keep on puffing, so you can keep being told: "you're not welcome here any more" — which should **really** put a smile on that glowing face of yours!

5) The minute you quit, you begin reversing the process of tar accumulation that's been going on for 10 or 20 years. No problem with that, except it will usually mean an **increase** in coughing, as the little cells in your lungs start bringing up more and more of the nearly-solid, gray-brown clumps of crud that have been biding their time down there, just **waiting** to turn your

lungs into killing lumps of cancerous coal (oops — there we go with that "C" word again! Can't believe we let it slip out! Strike that from the record, would you? Thanks!)

In all seriousness: if you don't think you'll be able to tolerate this **increase** in coughing (no matter that it's now because something **good** is happening!), but would prefer to simply stay with the delicate little cough you've come to know and love (what we used to call "Smoker's Cough" till some Smokers' Rights organization had the term stricken from the record), then the **last** thing you'll want to do is quit!

So don't!

6) The minute you quit, your house and car will start smelling as bad to you as they've smelled to everyone else the last 20 years.

The solution to this "rude awakening?"

Obviously:

> Get **rid** of the house and car; or
>
> **Clean** the house and car; or
>
> Start smoking again, so everything will once again smell the way it always used to.

Our advice on this one?

Spic n' Span.

And now that we've reviewed most of the "cons" of quitting, what about the "pros?"

Well, there are obviously an awful lot of them, and it would take a lot of space to go into them all. So maybe we can condense them for you just a little bit:

LIFE

10
...of the Yankees

Yes, we know: you're **proud** of the fact that you smoke! In a world where it's so difficult to accomplish **anything**, you're proud of the fact that you can put a cigarette in the corner of your mouth exactly where it's supposed to go; proud of the fact that you can light it up in wind conditions that would keep tall ships at bay; proud that you can pull the smoke into your mouth and lungs like a real pro and blow it out again in a way that never fails to make prospective lovers go weak in the knees!

Yes, there's a lot you can be proud of. And the funny thing is: the more you get dumped on for your habit — the more non-smoking restaurants, theaters and plane flights they sneak in on you while you're out having a smoke — the **prouder you get** — a fact not lost on the folks at Philip Morris, who are behind you a million per cent in your fight to **stay** proud!

No problem with this, except when you decide you want to **quit** smoking; then stuff starts hitting the fan.

Why?

Because there are so **few** things in our lives that any of us can be proud of, it doesn't sit well with our Subconscious Mind when we tell it we're going to be getting rid of the one thing that's our **main** source of pride: smoking! Which is why it fights us tooth-and-nail, every time we try to do that.

How to get around this?

Easy: **Don't** try to "get around it!" That's right: since your Subconscious will **never** let you take away its Number One source of pride without a fight, **don't** try to take it away!

Instead, try to **increase** your sense of pride!

How?

By going back to the mirror you spent so much time in front of when you were 12 or 13 and doing all the things you did back then to become a good smoker, but doing them even better now, using every drop of the 20 or 30 years' **more** experience at doing them you've managed to accumulate!

That's right: making a cigarette pop out of the pack with an even more subtle flick of your wrist than you could manage at 12; putting that cigarette into your mouth in the most artistically-satisfying corner you can find (if you need help figuring out where that is, just check with any of the hundreds of cigarette billboards and magazine ads your children gape at every day); lighting that cigarette in a way that will make the world forget Bogie and Bette once and for all!; taking a massive drag into your mouth the way it **should** be taken — not the way a geek or wimp would take it (especially a non-**smoking** geek or wimp) — and then Frenching the smoke up through your nose, because "there really **is** no other way;" then holding the smoke in your lungs for as long as anyone ever has, at no time giving any indication that that smoke is bringing you anything but pleasure; and then exhaling it as if it's been the most enjoyable experience of your life, which, when the nicotine hits your brain, it will be!

How did that feel? Great, huh?

In fact, why stop there? You want "pride?;" we can give you "pride:"

Take a gallon of Johnnie Walker Red to your mirror, along with a shot glass, and................no, wait: try this:

Get a "base pipe" from your cocaine-smoking neighbor before his heart explodes and take **that** to your mirror and............Oh, no, no, no: I've got it:

Stop the junkie who's breaking into your grandmother's house and ask to borrow his spoon and his needle and his rubber hose and his matches and take **those** to your mirror and.................no, wait:................

11
Cookie Cutter

But I don't **want** to give up smoking and be like everybody else!"

And you're right: all non-smokers **are** cut from the same mold: There are no artists among them, no writers, no poets, no musical geniuses, no sportsmen, no actors or actresses, no life-saving doctors, no crusading lawyers — none of those! Just a bunch of civil engineers who could no more hold a conversation than they could the ash from your cigarette.

So you're **right** not to want to be like them!
And, if you keep puffing your guts out the way you **have** been, you won't have to worry about **becoming** like them for very much longer!

Glad we could help you out of **that** nightmare!

Look, before you stop yourself from quitting because of all the "bad" things that not smoking has to offer, remember this:

IF YOU DON'T LIKE YOUR LIFE AS A NON-SMOKER, YOU CAN ALWAYS START SMOKING AGAIN!

As much as I'd like to wipe Philip Morris and R. J. Reynolds from the face of this planet (and, I am sure, they me!), I'll consider it an overwhelming victory if I can manage to put so much as a tiny **scuff** on the cover of their Annual Report!

So, you can take it from me: the minute you want to go back to your habit, old Phil and R. J. will be right there, hat in hand, to greet you — maybe even throw you a little party, maybe even a necktie party — you know: where everybody gets dressed up and rides around in limousines.

(Excuse me? That's what I said: "Black tie party." What? Well, what's the difference: "**black** tie," "**neck**tie!" It's the **party** I'm talking about!)

So don't for a minute think that giving up smoking is some kind of **death** sentence that no Governor on **Earth** could commute! Not at all! In fact, it's just the opposite: if ever there was an **easier** sentence to "overturn," I can't imagine it! I mean, what does it take: a couple of bucks and a Bicful of butane and you're right back where you started: in that delightful nicotine coma that bears such a striking resemblance to those **other** popular comas — you know: the ones from cocaine and heroin and booze!

So for God's sake, don't worry:

If you can't stand the thought of waking up with clear lungs, or of walking twice as fast and twice as far as you ever could, or of watching those nicotine-filled trunks under your eyes start to vanish, or of having skin that **won't** make your undertaker's pulse race, or of never again being told you "can't eat here" and you "can't fly there," or of being forced to associate with the billions of "losers" who **don't** smoke — if none of that appeals to you, no problem: **start smoking again**! No one's going to stop you! No one **can**!

All we're saying is: just **try** the non-smoking life for a little while.

Why?

For one reason: so that, when it comes time to decide whether you want to **continue** not smoking or to start back **up** again, the choice you make will for once be an **intelligent** one: "OK: this is what **smoking** has to offer and this is what **not** smoking has to offer, so let's see: which one do I want?"

If you never know what it's like **not** to smoke, then what kind of "choice" could you claim to be making when you say "I'll play these!"?

And if, after being off cigarettes for a respectable period of time, you do decide to start smoking again? No problem: At least it will be **your** decision this time, and not Philip Morris's or Humphrey Bogart's or your mom and dad's — or whichever smoking role model you couldn't wait till puberty to pattern yourself after!

Is it good, to know that it's **you** making the choice this time and not some heavily-limousined advertising agency? Well, just ask someone who **never** got to choose the course his life would take — whose every step was programmed **for** him — and see how happy **he** is (better bring along plenty of hankies!)

So, if you quit for no other reason, at least quit for that one: so that, if you ever start back up again, you'll at least have gotten to know how the "other half" lives and be able to state, **without reservation**, that you **don't want to live that way**! In other words, you'll be making an **informed** decision this time, and not the "blind" decision you've always let Phil and R. J. and Bogie make **for** you!

And if you **never** quit? Of course: then how will you ever know **who** you're smoking for?!

12
The Buddy System

If cigarettes are nothing else, they're your friend, your "buddy." And every time you light up, you **renew** this friendship, you reaffirm its solidity, its eternal nature: "Pals forever!"

It's the "chumminess" of smoking — the warm feeling you get when you hold your tiny friend in your little hand — that makes it so hard to quit the habit. After all: who has so many friends that he can afford to just toss one away?!

Now, we **could** go into all the things this glorious friendship is costing you: your health; the respect of others (luckily, it hasn't put a serious dent in your **self**-respect yet, though for the life of us we don't know **why**!); lost job opportunities; etc. — but why bother, since **you** could tell **us** what your habit is costing you as easily as we could tell you, so why waste the paper?

No: you know exactly what your friendship is costing you and, since you choose to continue it in the face of such onrushing disaster, does that give you a clue as to just how strong a friendship it is?!

Is it, in fact, **too** strong? Can it never be dealt with? Well, it won't be easy, but yes: it can be dealt with. How?

Well, why is that cigarette your "little buddy" in the first place?

Because it does for you all the things **any** friend would do:

1) It calms you down in times of trouble;

2) It touches you and you touch it — with your hands and with your lips;

3) It's always there for you when you need it — especially late at night, on a lonely road or in a lonely room.

In other words: it **is a friend**!

But it also happens to be killing you, which should never be Job One for **anything** you call "friend!"

So, as good a friend as it is — and all you have to do is watch the love affair people have with their cigarettes to know just how good a friend that is — it's a friend that, sad to say, has to be sent away, since the longer it stays, the less time you'll be around to enjoy it — which could prove a real inconvenience to all your **life-size** friends!

What to do? How to get rid of a buddy you've gotten so used to?

Again: it's not easy; but it can be done.

The first thing you have to do, of course, is convince yourself that your friend has to go away. Until you've done that, your chances of actually **sending** it away are pretty slim. So take however long you need to, to accept the fact that cigarettes are about to leave your life (try imagining they're a cancer you can get rid of by just wishing it away and see if that helps.)

O. K., so that's done. Now, how do you go about actually pushing your friend out the door?

Well, there are a lot of ways:

1) Visualize yourself as a non-smoker; see yourself **not** smoking at all those points in time when you used to light up without even thinking about it.

What to do instead?

Of course: **celebrate** your new life by **using** those lungs that you used to destroy! That's right: "breathe" where you used to "drag!" (Luckily, you should be able to do this wherever you want, since very few restaurants and the like have non-**breathing** sections!)

2) Create your own list of all the bad things smoking does to you (we could do it for you, but it will mean more if it comes from your own head and hand).

Of course, if you're one of those folks using smoking to commit slow **suicide**, this list will have an effect exactly **opposite** to the one we're looking for, but that's a chance we'll just have to take.

Anyway, once this list of bad things is done, go over it as often as you need to, to make all the things on it as much a part of your life as the **good** things about smoking ever were (if you need to refresh yourself on what those good things are, just go back to the list you got from the American Tobacco Institute last Christmas).

If you're lucky, it won't take very long for the list of horrors to work its "magic" and get you wondering why you ever thought cigarettes were such a "bargain" in the first place!

And if you're **not** so lucky? Then the list won't do a thing. At which point, you might consider writing something else — something along the lines of who you want to get what!

3) Since smoking is such a "touching" thing — the cigarette nestled in your fingers, then caressing your lips, then being "flicked" by thumb or forefinger — losing this constant touching may be the very thing that keeps you from quitting.

The solution? Easy: **Don't** lose it! Instead, get something just **like** a cigarette, that you can nestle in your fingers, caress with your lips, etc.

Yes, we hear you: "Those things never work!"

Well, of course they "never work!" But do you know why?

"No."

Because people try using **them** to get off cigarettes!

So what?

So, no piece of plastic ever invented can overcome a lifetime of physical and psychological addiction!

The way you overcome an addiction is by convincing the brain that's **addicted** that it **shouldn't** be!; that to get the addiction going, you had to **do** something to yourself — it wasn't something that just happened naturally — which means you can just as easily **un**do it!

Once your brain — specifically: your Subconscious Mind — understands that, the battle is all but over.

At **that** point in time, if a piece of plastic will help you overcome a **final** hurdle, then by all means **use that plastic** (or piece of candy or gum). But never use it — or think it **can** be used — to overcome the **first** hurdle — or any hurdle in between!

The bottom line is: there are a lot of ways to get your little buddy out of your life. And all of them share at least one important feature: they all allow you to put "distance" between you and your last cigarette.

Why is that so important?

Because nothing can loosen cigarettes' deadly grip on you more effectively than going without them for a week or two. In fact, all it **takes** is time, to show you that that cigarette was never your friend to begin with, even though it **was** there when no one else was, and it was warm and glowing and cute and cuddly, so how could you **not** think of it as a friend?!

Yes, we know: It comforted you through many a lonely night.

Well, so would a toothpick, if you'd just given it a chance (remember: we're talking "friendship" here; not "drugs.")

Believe us: there's nothing so "magical" about a cigarette's "friendship" that it can't be replaced — unless you consider the sedation nicotine gives you and the cancer you get from tar to be "magical," at which point we're no longer talking "**friendship**" any more!

So why not try breaking off this "friendship" as soon as you can? We think you'll thank yourself for doing so.

And if you don't? If you miss your friend so much that you "can't wait" to get him back?! No problem: **Get him back**! He won't be sleeping under a freeway overpass somewhere where you can't find him, like all the **other** friendless people in this world! Oh no: he'll be sitting warm and cozy-like, in every store that could even **remotely** justify selling him!

Heck: your greatest worry on Earth should be "not finding and getting reunited with your favorite smokes!"

And if you can't make it out to the store? No problem: Just call one of your **life-size** friends — preferably one who smokes (and, if you're an ex-smoker, most do) — and tell **him** what you need! I'm sure he'll be more than happy to bring you over a **carton** of little buddies — help make the "reunion" one for "all time" — or at least for as much time as those "buddies" decide to give you.

So no: Don't ever think you're giving up your friends for good.

All we're saying is: Just make sure they **are** your friends, before you go inviting them back into your house again. Because if they're not, you may find them taking more than just the silverware with them, the **next** time they leave!

13
It's Impossible

Of course, let's not kid ourselves: Because there are so many things pushing you **toward** cigarettes and so very few telling you to stay **away** from them, the chances that any of you will ever quit for good are pretty remote.

Then why bother?

Because saving **one** in a million from slavery is always better than saving **none** in a million.

Not a big enough difference to be worth the effort? Try telling that to her kids!

So, no: we don't really hold out much hope for very many of you. And here's why:

1) As a smoker, you spend so much of your life around **other** smokers — at work, in restaurants, in bars, at ballgames, playing cards, etc. — that even if you **did** quit, you'd still be surrounded by such a dense cloud of smoke all day that, without even getting **close** to flicking your Bic, you'd wind up smoking about two packs a day anyway!

Why so many? Because remember: the smoke you inhale from someone **else's** cigarette is coming at you "full strength!"; it hasn't had the benefit of a cigarette's-worth of tobacco and a filter's-worth of carboxymethylcellulose to leach out most of its chemical "bite!" So even though you're not taking the massive "hit" every 30 seconds that the smoker is, your continuous **little** hits can add up to at least as much nicotine and tar in **your** lungs (and everywhere else in your body) as he's getting in his.

Also: he's only smoking his cigarette every 30 seconds; you're "smoking" it **every second it's lit** (yes, we hear you: "He's breathing the same air!" Well, normally he would be, except for one thing: "Murphy's Law of Non-smokers:" "No matter where a non-smoker sits, he will always be directly in the path of any and all smoke!" Thus, you will **always** get more of a smoker's "unfiltered" smoke than he will. In other words, you're **not** really breathing the same air! Sorry!)

So even though you never let a cigarette get near your lips, as long as you keep hanging around with people who do you'll be "smoking" as much as you ever have. So what reason would you have for quitting, and depriving yourself of the wonderful **ritual** of smoking — tapping the pack, flicking out the cigarette, lighting your lighter, setting fire to the cigarette, taking a drag, being "cool," etc. — when there's nothing to be gained health-wise from doing so?!

The solution? Of course: Give up all the smoking friends you've had for the last 20, 30 years and start hanging around with a **new** crowd. Or just stop **breathing** when you're around that "old gang of yours!"

Either way: good luck!

2) If you smoke, there's a good chance your spouse does, too.

So what?

So when you quit, you take the biggest step you could possibly take toward becoming a winner.

So what?

So that makes everybody who didn't take that step **with** you look like an even **bigger** "loser" than he or she already was!

So what?

So you have to **live** with that loser and the more of a loser your spouse looks to be — the more your strength "exposes" his or her weakness — the unhappier you'll make his or her life, since very few people do cartwheels at the thought of being looked on as "weak" or a "loser."

Now I don't know about you, but I'm not all that crazy about doing things that turn my wife into the world's "unhappiest camper" (though I somehow manage to cram in about a hundred of those things every day before breakfast!)

So, in the interests of keeping the home fires **lit** — forget "burning!" — most quitters take the easy way out and just start smoking again, which restores family unity with a minimum of grief (until, of course, the biopsy results come back).

How to get around this dilemma?
Naturally: have both spouses quit at the same time.
Great solution!: If the odds of a single person quitting are one in a million, you want to quote me the odds, not only of **two** people quitting, but of two people quitting **at the same time**!
Forget it: your calculator doesn't go that high!

Another solution?
Of course: Just keep on smoking.

Care to guess which one the majority of you married smokers will be taking?

3) As mentioned in several other places: smoking is so much a part of **everything** you do that quitting the habit would be like throwing out a **hundred** "babies" with a single tub of (yellow) "bathwater!" Since the thought of such a mass "slaughter" is just too appalling to even consider, you don't need anyone twisting your arm **not** to consider it. Meaning: you don't need anyone to convince you to keep right on smoking!

4) Again: you're **proud** of your habit; **proud** that you can inhale hot, stinging smoke when so few of your former playmates can; **proud** that you're now able to do what you always **wanted** to do, for as long as you can remember: act just like your mommy or daddy or all your buddies or all your heroes of the silver screen.

The fact is: We all have to be proud of something. And, since you apparently have so little **else** to be proud of, you'll be **damned** if you're going to give up the one thing that **does** make your chest puff out!

So you don't!

5) No matter how hard you try — and no matter how ugly that stuff looks, swimming around in the toilet after your morning "coughathon" — you just can't convince yourself that smoking is anything more than a "harmless diversion!"

And, since it **is** so harmless, what reason would you have for giving it up?

So you don't!

Obviously, we could go on with this forever. But you get the picture: Everywhere you look, the world seems to be telling you just one thing: Keep on smoking! Which is why so few of you will ever do anything **but**; will ever take the week or two you need, to make smoking something the "**other** guy" does!

Does that mean that **none** of you ever will? No. It just means that we won't be needing an IBM mainframe to keep track of our success rate!

Should that "stop" us?

Well, eight years ago, I was one of those lucky enough to **beat** the odds, and if I can pass along some of that "luck" to you, hey: how ticked off can St. Peter get?!

So, no: low success rate doesn't bother me: if "one in a million" is all I can get, then "one in a million" will just have to do for now.

And how do I keep my spirits up, in the face of such an abysmally-low number? Easy: With the thought that I'm talking to that one in a million **right now**!

Am I?

14
Watch Out!

If you do manage to beat the odds and quit smoking, there's one pitfall you must always, always, always avoid! It usually goes something like this:

"Well, it looks like I've kicked my smoking habit. And since I have, and since it went so smoothly, it probably wasn't that big a thing to do in the first place. Which means the habit, itself, couldn't have been that big a **deal** in the first place — just like they always claimed it wasn't. Which means I can probably go back to having a cigarette every now and then — after work, say, or after dinner, or after the kids are in bed — but with **me** controlling **it** this time, instead of the other way around!"

Sure; and maybe Stalin could have figured out a way to kill only a **few** peasants every year, instead of a few **million**!

Forget it! There **is** no such thing as keeping a cigarette habit "under control" — unless, of course, you're one of those rare birds who's been smoking only one or two cigarettes a day for the last 30 years or so and has never felt a need for any more. At which point, all we can say is: We hate your guts and why the hell are you reading this book?!

For the rest of you — the ones like me, who, when asked why I kept lighting one cigarette off another, would carefully (and cutely) explain that I was participating in a "butane conservation program" (hey: **some** of them "bought" it!) — forget it:

you have one cigarette today, after you've been off them for a week or a month or even a year, and I guarantee you you'll be back up to two packs a day before you can breathe!

Trust me: you're either a "smoker" or a "non-smoker;" you will never be a "controlled" smoker, no matter how much Philip Morris and R. J. Reynolds try to convince you you can be (only smoke when you're fishing; only smoke when you're branding steers; only smoke when you're visiting another addict's new apartment; etc.!)

If you **get** off cigarettes, **stay** off cigarettes! Don't **ever** think you can go back on them at anything less than "full tilt," because, if you do, the only things you'll be "tilting" will be tons of cash into Philip Morris's drawers and yourself into an early grave!

Get the picture?

15
Yes, Dahling!

I was just thinking: You know, it's incredible how much sophistication smoking can give you — and with nothing more than the flick of your Bic!

That's right: by simply setting fire to a plant, you can get as sophisticated, as worldly, as anyone who's ever walked the Earth!

Don't think that's miraculous? Then name me one other thing that can give you **any** kind of sophistication without your having to actually **do** something to get it:

Like your chances of becoming a gourmet cook without ever **tasting** anything?; an art connoisseur without ever looking at a painting?; a judge of "good sex" by never sleeping with anyone but yourself?

And yet, that's exactly what smoking gives you: the instant you light up, you become one of those fancy-dressed men and women in the magazine ads, dancing the night away at a Presidential Ball, or relaxing in ritzy clubs or drop-dead-gorgeous apartments, talking their sophisticated talk and living their sophisticated lives, with cigarettes dangling from their fingers and smoke trailing dreamily from their lips every minute they're alive!

Wow—too bad high school wasn't this easy; you could've been a lawyer by now!

And let's not forget how **"worldly"** smoking makes you — without the hideous expense of actually leaving your front porch!

The instant you light up, you are "at one" with every Frenchman, Italian, German and every **other** world-class sophisticate you can think of who's lighting up at the same time you are, thousands of miles away!

I don't know about you, but I used to get a goosey feeling in my stomach, knowing there were so many with-it people around the world who had discovered the same secret to eternal pleasure that I had (well, OK: the secret that the American Tobacco Company **helped** me discover. But it was **my** decision to do it, so that really makes it **my discovery**, when you get right down to it!)

And the nice thing is: it's so simple to **see** this sophistication, this worldliness in action.

By going all the way to Europe?

Not at all!

Then where?

Of course: in any downtown park, where a cigarette dangles constantly from the sophisticated lips of all the General Pattons and Clara Bartons in the Army of the Hopeless.

16
"...with a stick!"

One of the great comforts for any cigarette addict is the knowledge that

Smoking causes lung cancer and, if you don't get that, you've beaten the game!

And it would probably be even **more** comforting if it were true!

"It's not?!"

No.

"But—"

Yes, I know: smoke goes into the lungs and comes out of the lungs. So, as long as the lungs stay "cool," **you** should stay "cool."

"Right!"

Just one question:

"What?"

Are the lungs the **only** place the smoke goes to?

"Well, sure!"

It doesn't stop in the mouth at all?

"Well, maybe for an instant..."

Right. And how much time do you think all those little cancer-causing chemicals need, to dive into your saliva and start doing some heavy, white-water rafting down your gullet and into your stomach, small intestine, large intestine, kidneys, bladder, liver?

"'Not much?'"

Not much. And, if those chemicals can turn your lungs into a cancerous mess, what's to stop them from doing the same to the rest of you?

"'Prayer?'"

Bingo!

Before I wised up, I used to think it was sheer coincidence that smokers were coming down with a lot more than just lung cancer; I figured all those other cancers could just as easily have been due to something they ate or to some genetic defect or maybe sunspots (luckily, the American Tobacco Institute was able to back me up with hardcopy on all three!).

But one day, as I was kissing my yearly set of deliciously-"clear" chest X-rays, a single word popped into my head — "saliva" — and I stopped my "love-in" and immediately started wondering what might be going on everywhere **else** in the old bod!

And, even though it's been a medically-uneventful eight years since I quit, I'm **still** wondering. And will **always** be wondering!

And praying!

So...what will **you** be doing, the next eight years?

17
The Family Plot

As I watched my Aunt Lillian lying comatose in an iron lung at the age of 46, the victim of a massive stroke that couldn't have been **helped** by her three-pack-a-day Pall Mall habit, I was confident that, if there was any consciousness left in that incredibly-lifeless form, it was screaming out for a cigarette at that very moment (a few hours later, it was no longer screaming out for anything).

Or the picture of my Aunt Esther, as **she** lay near death from a Lucky Strike habit that had all but dissolved her heart muscle: pulling my mother close to her in those last hours and whispering, not the secret of life, but the fact that she was "dying for a cigarette" (an analysis of the situation that was far closer to the truth than she would ever have admitted) and would my mother see what she could do about getting her one.

Naturally, my mother could do nothing — except go out into the waiting room and have a cigarette herself, to ease the immense grief she felt at not being able to get her sister one.

As an aside: it has always been a mystery to me, and will always **be** a mystery to me, why doctors feel it's critical to deprive a terminal patient of something he or she enjoys — even if that "something" is the reason the patient is "terminal!" Do the doctors think that by doing so they are adding something measurable to the lifespan of people like my aunt, who didn't have more than a week left anyway?

Why do they do it? So they can pin more medals on their chest for being "good doctors?"

Do they ever — did they ever — stop to consider the havoc they are wreaking by asking people on their deathbed to suddenly give up something they may have been doing every day of their adult lives?

What does it prove? And who benefits?

And if no one benefits, why do it?!

As someone who was very deeply involved with the medical profession before running from it in horror, let me answer my own question:

No: they never consider the impact their "life-saving decision" might be having on the mental well-being of the patient. To them, everything is black-and-white: "'Smoking' is bad; 'not smoking' is good," so have the smoker stop smoking.

Will that add a minute or two onto the smoker's life? Perhaps. Will that minute be a comfortable one? Don't ask!

Will this incredibly-cruel attitude ever change? Not as long as we keep insisting that our doctors are "gods" and those doctors keep nodding!

The moral of the story? Take smoking away from yourself while it's still **your** choice, because if you let others make the choice for you, you'll wind up wanting to take everybody in white over to the "other side" **with** you!

And now: back to our story...

...and my father, who never wore anything but two-pocket shirts, and it wasn't because of any **Chiclets** habit: convincing himself that he was doing nothing more each day than administering a harmless little sedative to himself — about 96 times **more** each day than the harm**ful** kind would have required — until we finally changed his forwarding address, once and for all!

Why bring this up? Because these were all such sterling individuals that they deserved to live forever?

Well, no: only one person's ever been **that** sterling. But yes: the world is a far, far poorer place without them.

Can I bring them back?

No. But I can keep you from joining them before your "time."

Or rather: you can keep **yourself** from joining them, since I can't do a thing for you that you don't already want to do for yourself!

The "bottom line" — now and forever?:

The same as it was for all the dearly-departed in my **own** family: It's your move!

18
Winners and Losers

As with so many other things in life, all we're really talking about here is "winning" versus "losing."

Should make life pretty simple, shouldn't it:

If what you're doing is making you a "winner," keep on doing it; if what you're doing is making you a "loser," **stop** doing it!

Simple, huh? Should make "losers" about as hard to find as passenger pigeons or middle-aged dinosaurs.

And are they?

I don't know; why don't you look around you? What do you see? Me, too: people who

- smoke
- drink
- overeat
- watch endless hours of mindless TV
- do drugs
- gamble
- brutalize their children
- work as little as possible
- etc.

See any "winners" in that group? Me neither.

And all we can wonder is: why not? When it's so simple to be a "winner," why do these people continue to make themselves "losers?"

Because its "**fun**" being a loser?

Well, yes: all those things do provide a certain amount of "fun" — at least in the short run. But, when you consider the long-term consequences of such short-term "fun," you have to wonder why anyone over the age of 12 would want to **keep** doing any of them!

And yet, they **do**, so there's obviously something **else** going on here.

What else?

Simply this: somewhere in the long ago, each of these losers "bought" someone else's "line" — usually an advertising agency's but just as often a friend's or relative's — that doing any or all of those things would make him, not a "**loser**," but a "**winner**!"

That's right:

- "Smoking is 'cool!'"; "cool" people are "winners;"
- "Drinking is 'adult'"; "being adult" is "cool;"
- "You can eat your sorrows away!"; "unsorrowful people" are "happy people" and "happy people" are "winners;"
- "You have a God-given **right** to be entertained 24 hours a day!"; people getting what's due them are always "winners;"
- "The world's a crummy place; there's nothing wrong with using drugs to escape from it!"; doing something that's "not wrong" is the same as doing something that's "right," which always makes you a "winner;"
- "Winning the lottery or the million-dollar slots means you'll never have to work again for the rest of your life!"; people who never have to work are "winners;"
- "There's nothing wrong with getting children to toe the line — no matter what it takes to do that!"; parents with totally-behaved children are "winners;"
- "Half of what I make goes to the government anyway, so why should I work any harder just to make **them** rich?"; people who keep the government from getting any richer are automatic "winners;"
- and on and on.

But it doesn't end there:

"Losing" things can only be portrayed as "winning" things for just so long; then, their true nature leaks out and they're finally seen for the losing propositions they always were.

So, where does that leave the person whose life is **based** on those things? After all: none of us can live with the thought of being a "loser." And yet, there we are, trapped in a losing situation.

How to get out of such a mess? Of course: **Go on the offensive**! Find even **more** ways to "prove" that what you're doing is making you a "winner!"

And how do you do that?

Well, let's see how smokers do it:

• The same drug — nicotine — that everyone else knows is **killing** him, due to its ability to squeeze off blood flow to every part of his body, is, in the smoker's eyes, actually **improving** his life, since cutting off the blood flow to his brain has a "calming" effect, which makes him better able to "function" (after all: what good to the world is a "bundle of nerves?")

• The habit that is making him **less and less** desirable to have around — in restaurants, airplanes, theaters and the like — is, he still believes, making him **more** desirable, since it's making him "cool," "worldly" and "sophisticated" and **everyone** wants to spend time with those kinds of people, if given the chance to. So, all our smoker has to do is sit tight, keep smoking and just wait for everyone else to "see the light."

• The habit that's **killing** him, due to its easy ability to give birth to cancers all over his body, is, he will tell you, actually **extending** his life by keeping him thin, since "We all know the grim 'numbers' on fat people!"

• The same cigarette he needs to suck on, the way a baby sucks on a pacifier, is, he is convinced, proving conclusively to the world how **adult** he is, since "babies don't smoke!"

—and on and on, with one good reason after another why a habit that everybody else knows is making him a "loser" is, in fact, making him as big a "winner" as ever walked the Earth! Tell me we won't go to any lengths........!

And please don't think we're picking on smokers here. Oh no! This "loser-into-winner" miracle is **everywhere**!:

• Gamblers who are struck dumb when you tell them the odds against winning the lottery: "As long as **one** person wins it," they'll answer, "what do I care about all the jerks who **don't**?! Talk about a '**loser**!'" as he walks away from you, shaking his head;

• The alcoholic who can point to one beer commercial after another — where vibrant, young folks are having more fun than the rest of the planet put together — and shout, before passing out: "How bad could something be that can do **that** for people?!"

Again: the examples are endless.

Will this situation ever change?

Well, as long as "losers" can prove beyond a shadow of a doubt that they're "winners," why in God's name would they **change**?!:

• As long as drunks can "prove" that if they drink enough beers, they, too, will be magically transported to some desert oasis — where unbelievably gorgeous women will desire them more than life, itself — why would they **stop** drinking?

• As long as the State Lottery Commission can keep advertising its "game" as a "fun" thing you "play" — the same way you played with blocks in kindergarten — what reason would people who should never get within an **area code** of a Lottery booth suddenly have for not spending their last dollar "playing" it?!

No: losers will **always** be able to show you how "winning" a life they're leading — or at most are a few **days** from leading — so why would they change?

So don't think we're expecting you to suddenly see smoking as the most losing thing you can do! You think it's making you a "winner?" Fine: we won't keep trying to burst your bubble!

In fact, we'll stop harping on it and just close with a list of all the **other** people in the "smokers-are-winners" parade who couldn't agree with you more:

• R. J. Reynolds
• Liggett & Myers
• P. Lorillard
• The American Tobacco Company
• Their advertising agencies
• Their bankers
• Their shareholders
• Their cancer doctors
• Their heart doctors
• Their lung doctors
• Your undertaker.

19
Sniff

We know you're amazed when everybody complains about the vomitaceous smell in your house, your clothes, your hair, your car, your office, your dog. After all, **you** can't smell anything — at least nothing you'd call "**unpleasant**" — so what is it that everybody's making such a big fuss about?!

You really want to know? Then take your ashtray, empty it out, bury your nose in it and **smell**! Does that answer your question?!

"But—"

No "buts" about it: what **you** smelled is what **we** smell, every time we're within a zip code or two of your home planet!

"But we don't bury your head in our ashtray!"

You don't have to: what you smelled in that ashtray is what we smell from Mars!

They why do **you** have to go to such extremes to get the same effect?

Because your nose has become so paralyzed to the "normal" smell of cigarettes that the only way you can **smell** that "normal" smell is by breaking through that paralysis!

How?

By bombarding your "smellers" with "everything you've got!" Thus, the "ashtray facial!"

Will knowing that you and everything around you smells like an ashtray get you to stop smoking? Does driving into walls get the average alcoholic to stop drinking?

No: the drug and the habit and the sociability of smoking are such an unbeatable combination that nothing as puny as "bad smell" will ever come **close** to breaking it!

Then how **do** you bring down this mighty fortress?

The same way you bring down **any** fortress: one brick at a time — until the fortress collapses under its own weight, even though it still **looks** pretty strong, right to the bitter end.

The most **important** "brick," of course, is the one labeled: "Yagottawanna." It's the one that **gets** you smoking every day, so until it's safely in hand, it's the one that's going to **keep** you smoking every day!

And how do you get to that key brick? Obviously: by clearing away all the other bricks that help support it; you know, the ones labeled: "coolness," "worldliness," "sophistication," "sedation," "friendship" and so forth.

And what happens when you've got all **those** bricks in hand, including the one you were **really** going for: "Yagottawanna?" Well first, you turn them over, to see what they have on their "flip sides." And what do you see? Of course: "cancer" and "heart disease" and "stroke" and "emphysema" and "endless cough" and on and on and on.

And what do you do after you've turned them over and seen them for what they really are? Of course: you build a **new** fortress with them — one that will keep smoking **out** of your life as surely as the old fortress kept it **in**!

And **will** this new fortress be just as strong as the old one?

Don't know, until you start building it — one brick at a time.

And while you've got your hardhat on...

You have to remember one thing: What you're trying to do here is nothing less than build a new life for yourself, because smoking is so much a part of your **current** life that there's just no easy way of "fixing" it; you simply have to start over.

Frightening?

Perhaps.

But you want to see "frightening?" Look at your lungs!

Can we make it **less** frightening? In a heartbeat:

You build a new life the same way you build a new house: one brick at a time.

In the case of a life, the "bricks" are "hours:" every hour that you **live** right builds you a life that **is** "right." No big deal, right?

Well, here **is** the big deal:

When you build a house, you don't have to keep laying the same brick over and over again, which would find you laying bricks forever! Oh no: Once a brick is laid, it's laid, and every one of those bricks you lay brings you one brick closer to the day when you'll have **no** more bricks to lay — at which point, all you'll have left to do is admire your new house!

It's the same thing when you're building a new life: Every hour that you can do without something is a "brick" that never has to be laid again; put enough of those "bricks" together and what you wind up with is a completely changed life — without you having to do anything more to keep it that way!

In other words: if you want to quit smoking, you may have to actually **push** the cigarettes away for a week or so; but if you **can** do that, that's all the pushing away you'll ever have to do, because there won't be anything pushing you **to** them after that: your "non-smoking 'house'" will be completely built and all **you'll** have to do is "**live**" in it!

Remember and remember well:

You're not giving up cigarettes forever;
You're only giving up cigarettes for a few **days**!

It's your Subconscious **Mind** that's giving them up forever, right after you "tell" it that's what you want it to do!

And how do you do that? Of course: by giving up cigarettes for a few days!

And why does that work?

Because each cigarette you **don't** smoke is not only one less cigarette you **do** smoke but one less cigarette you **will** smoke, because of the powerful signal not smoking it gives to your Subconscious Mind: "I want you to make **not** smoking as much of a 'habit' as **smoking** ever was!"

And your Subconscious will!

At which point, you will automatically **become** a non-smoker, which you definitely **can't** become until your Subconscious Mind lets you!

Now, I don't know about you, but if someone told me that all I'd have to do, to change my whole life around, is just change my life for a few **days**, at which point my mind and body would take over and keep the changes going **for** me, I'd have only one thing to say: "Where do I sign?!"

The better question, of course, is: Where do **you** sign?

And the answer is: Anywhere you want, and the sooner the better!

20
Mr. Excitement

What a fascinating life you lead:

Smoking all day Sunday;
Smoking all day Monday;
Smoking all day Tuesday;
Smoking all day Wednesday;
Smoking all day Thursday;
Smoking all day Friday;
Smoking all day Saturday;
Smoking all day Sunday;
Smoking all day Monday;
Smoking all day Tuesday

.
.
.
.
.

Why such an unbroken chain of thrills?

Because if there's one thing we humans absolutely can't stand it's "change:" we will do **anything** to avoid it!: stay with dead-end jobs, dead-end marriages, dead-end governments, dead-end habits, dead-end **everything**, if it means we'll never have to "change."

In fact, making a change is **so** terrifying that we will almost **always** prefer going down with a Hell-bound ship to jumping off into uncharted waters, even if that's the only chance we have of saving ourselves!

This is human nature; it's not about to change.

Oh, not that we humans **mind** change; in fact, we **love** it! It gives life meaning, vitality! It's just that we don't want to make the changes **ourselves**!

But let someone else make the changes **for** us? "Hey: no problem; we're with you guys a thousand per cent!" — most often, as it happens, because we have no choice in the matter, but that's beside the point.

Anyway, there's the situation: we don't **want** to change, yet we don't **resist** change when it's forced upon us.

The question is: Can we use these features of human nature to our advantage?

Well, knowing that you don't **want** to change makes it easier to understand why it's so **hard** to change, which should make you keep **trying** to change, long after you would normally have stopped, since you now know it's not as easy as it looked! So that's quite helpful.

And how can we use the knowledge that we won't **resist** change if it's forced upon us; that we'll always "waffle" and "go with the flow?"

In this way: Since no one else will force you to stop smoking (no one can!), what's wrong with forcing yourself? That's right: Pretend you're your own "critic" — someone completely apart from "yourself" — and tell yourself that the world is changing, that everybody with half a **brain** is giving up cigarettes, so you won't exactly be **alone** in your non-smokingness, and that your own life will be much, much better without the damn habit!

By imagining that someone **else** is forcing you to change, you relieve **yourself** of the burden of making that decision: "Well, I **have** to go along; they're **making** me!"

That's right: blame it on someone else, if that's what it takes!

And will that make it **easy** to change?

No.

After all, you could always count on cigarettes to comfort you in times of stress, to calm you down whenever your feathers got ruffled (even if you needed a microscope to make **sure** they had!)

Now, suddenly, your "old reliables" won't be there anymore; you won't be able to keep yourself under constant sedation — at least not with the deadliest, most enjoyable "sedative" yet devised!

What to do? Cry? Tear your clothing?

No. Just ask yourself why it is that half the world's population needs no sedative at all to make it through the day, and yet a few of those folks actually seem to be leading rather enjoyable, productive lives, so why can't you?!

No — forcing yourself to change by being your own cop won't make it **easy** to change. All it will do is make it easi**er**; and how long has it been since you were able to do **that** for yourself?!

21
Batter Up!

In baseball, when a team is going badly, it's always the manager who gets the ax, never the players — even though it's the players who are most responsible for winning or losing the game.

So why cut the manager loose?

Of course: because it's easier to fire **one** man than it is to fire **25**!

But there's more to it than that:

Even though the manager can't go out and play the game, he can definitely influence the way the other 25 guys play it. So even though it's true that he's "only one man," his influence is often far greater than such a small number would otherwise indicate.

So, it's **not** that crazy to assume that the manager's influence over the players is just as responsible for the team's losing streak as the players' lack of talent. Which means it's **not** that crazy to fire one man, when you'd really like to fire 25, because removing the influence of that one man can have the same effect — on paper at least — of firing those 25 players and hiring on 25 new ones.

And what effect does it have in "real life?" Of course: the same as it did "on paper:" with the old manager gone and a new guy at the helm, the players play like they've been given a new lease on life — which they have!: the team starts winning, the owner presents himself with a Genius of the Year Award and everybody looks forward to coming out to the old ballyard every day!

Until, one day, the new manager shoots himself in the foot by asking his players to concentrate even **more** out there: after all, he figures, if we're doing this well with them in a coma half the time, how much better **could** we be doing if some of these two-million-dollar-a-year guys actually paid **attention** when they were out in the field: covering a base when no one else can; going after a fly ball, even if the fielder it's hit to looks like a "lock" to catch it; moving a runner into scoring position so the **next** guy can bat him in, rather than trying to bring the runner all the way around from the **parking lot** yourself, by trying to hit the ball to East Jupiter — which usually gets the ball about as far out into the Solar System as the near end of the other team's dugout!?

And what is the end result of this new manager's outrageous demands? Of course: the same result the **old** manager got: a bunch of malcontents who've once again lost that "winning edge!"

Until, of course, this new manager is fired and.........and this is where we came in.

Why bring up a baseball story in a stop-smoking book?

For one reason: in the same way that a single manager can have an influence over 25 different players, and keep them from peforming their best, so one activity — smoking — can be an integral part of 25 different things you do each day; and, in the same way that it's easier to fire the manager than it is to fire 25 players, it's easier to keep smoking than it is to change 25 different activities all at once.

In the same way that it would frighten a team owner to death to have to replace 25 different players, rather than one single manager, so it frightens **you** to death to think of changing 25 different things all at once by taking away something that is so much a part of each of them!

So you **don't** take it away. And you're **not** "frightened to death!" Until your doctor finds it impossible to look you in the eye when he asks if you've got your financial house in order.

The fact is, we can't change this: smoking has woven itself so deeply into the fabric of your life that it might as well **be** your life. All we can tell you is that this is true for everyone: everyone who's ever given up smoking has had to face this same reality.

But you ought to face one other reality: even though smoking has been a part of everything you do for 10 or 20 or 30 years, the "healing power" of your own brain is so strong that if you can just find a way to do without those cigarettes for maybe a week or two, you can easily "break" the associations of an entire **lifetime**!

Is that a long time: a "week or two?"
Hard to say: depends on how long you plan to be dead.

22
Goals

If you're even a couple of years past grade school, we shouldn't have to tell you this, but we will anyway:

People who set goals and work toward them are more successful than people who don't.

Why bring that up here?

Because apparently a few of you never heard it — unless the aimless drifting you do, from one day to the next, is caused by a virus or something!

Trust us: There is nothing in life more important that setting a goal and working toward it. Nothing I know of (and I know a **lot**!) can turn a life around quicker and more completely than setting a goal and working toward it.

The main reason is: once the goal is set, the best path to get to it **lights up all by itself**, and all you have to do then is **walk** on it (well, almost)!

And what happens when you **don't** have a specific goal? That's right: No path, no lights, no action!

So the first thing you have to do, before you do **anything**, is make "not smoking" your goal!

And how do you do that?

Two ways:

1) Picture yourself as a non-smoker, doing all the things you've always done, just not in a cloud of toxic waste.

What will that do?

Let your Subconscious Mind know where you want it to take you.

2) Pass up as many smoking opportunities as you can each day.

What will that do?

Reinforce Number One.

Never forget: Your Subconscious Mind will take you wherever you tell it you want to go.

And how do you "tell" it that? By your own actions:

The more you smoke, the more it will **make** you smoke, thinking that it's doing you a favor; the less you smoke, the less it will think you **want** to smoke, and the **less** it will make you smoke, for the same reason.

The fact is: you design your own tomorrows by the things you do today. Abuse yourself today and you'll "need" to abuse yourself tomorrow; abstain from something today and you won't get as "hungry" for it tomorrow.

These are Laws of Nature; they can't be broken. You can either use them to **improve** your life or you can ignore them and keep wondering why your life has such a hard time getting out of the toilet!

It's your choice. Hope, for all concerned, that you'll choose wisely!

23
What's it to You?

As I was finishing a previous book (*Walk Yourself Thin*), overweight people started coming up to me and asking: "Hey: why do **you** care whether I'm fat or thin? I mean, what's it to you?! Why can't you just leave me alone and let me live my own life?!"

My answer to them was the same as it is to any of you **smokers** who might be wondering the same thing:

Because I have to live in your world.

And a world full of smokers is a world full of losers. And the bigger a loser **you** are, the bigger a loser you make **me**.

Why?

Because I have to

• breathe your smoke;

• pay, in one way or another, for your lung cancer, emphysema, heart disease, etc.;

• take care of your children when you leave them too early.

Not that I have anything against you personally, but I'd rather not do **any** of those things, if I can help it! I mean, I have my **own** pollution to worry about and my **own** diseases to pay for and my **own** kids to take care of, so I really don't need any more of those things from **you**!

And how do I **keep** you from pawning them off on me?

Of course: By getting you to stop smoking!

So I'm sorry if you thought I was doing all this for "noble" reasons, like one of those guys in shining armor. No way; it's completely selfish on my part: the minute I turn you from a loser into a winner, the minute I make my **own** life better, and that's all I care about!

Why?

Because I'm only going to be here once and why should I have to live that one life any closer to the gutter than I already am?!

So, no: there's nothing "noble" in what I'm doing. I want to get rid of your habit as selfishly as you want to hold on to it and inflict it on everyone else.

If **I** win, of course, we **both** win; if **you** "win".............

24
The First Week

OK, so you've decided to take the plunge: to replace a habit that's killing you — "smoking" — with one that won't: "not smoking."

Will your job be an easy one? As we've stated so many times throughout this book: No; change is **never** easy. All we can do is make it easi**er**.

And one of the ways to make it easier is to let you know what to expect when you stop smoking, since, unless the whole world changed while we were asleep, "knowledge" is "power," and, if you plan to get off cigarettes and **stay** off them, you'll need all the "power" you can get!

First, though, you have to understand that all the "changes" you'll be going through won't last forever, and will certainly be no more upsetting or painful than those first few drags were, ages and ages ago.

And what might those changes be?:

1) The first one will be a feeling of "abandonment," as the hole that cigarettes used to fill — when you awoke, when you ate, when you drove, when you phoned, when you walked, etc. — now lies there, gapingly **un**filled.

What to do?:

a) Remind yourself that that "hole" remains "unfilled" for about 4 billion **other** people every day and none of **them** seems to mind it all that much, so why should you?

84

b) Fill the "hole" with something **else** for a week or two. What else? **Anything** else!

2) If you drink coffee — and most smokers do, to counteract the mind-deadening effect of nicotine — you should be aware that, with your sedative gone, the caffeine will now have the run of the place! So what? Well, the minute caffeine no longer has to fight against nicotine to get some attention, it often starts acting like something Timothy Leary used to line up for; that's right: LSD.

And what "actions" might those be?

a) Tunnel vision, where it feels like you're looking at everything through cardboard tubes;

b Light flashes throughout your field of view;

c) Objects "moving" that are standing perfectly still;

d) A feeling like the top of your head is about to become the first living thing on Mars.

What to do?:

i) Be aware that these things could happen and just ride them out for a day or two;

ii) Give up coffee at the same time you're giving up cigarettes.

To that second suggestion, we have just a one-word response: "Ha!" Which might give you a clue as to which of the two you'll actually be doing!

3) You'll get a "gnawing" feeling in your gut, as your Subconscious Mind uses every "tool" at its disposal to get you smoking again — and "hitting you below the belt" is one of its all-time favorites, no matter **what** you're trying to give up!

What to do?:

Again: be aware that this is going to happen, but that it won't bother you for more than a day or two, and you want to point me out someone who can't ride out a little tummy churning for a "day or two?!"

4) You'll start to cough even **more** than when you were smoking, as your lungs **immediately** begin to reverse a lifetime of glop accumulation.

What to do?:

Cough! — but do it with the wonderful knowledge that every cough you cough is one less cough you'll **ever** cough, which should bring an even **bigger** smile to your lungs and things!

Remember: All these "changes" you'll be going through will only last for a little while. For the most part, they're your body's — and your brain's — last-gasp attempt to get you holding onto something they swore you **wanted** to hold onto, since you held onto it so **desperately** for all these years!

Once you "tell" them you **don't** want them holding onto the habit anymore —which you do by **not** lighting up every five minutes — they'll simply let go of it, with the same amount of passion they used to **embrace** it with!

But they won't do it — can't do it — until you "tell" them to do it.

How?

By laying down your smokes for a couple of days.

"That's it?"

That's it!

"Where do I sign?"

Same place as last time.

25
Murphy's Law

As with everything else in life, the minute you decide to quit smoking you run into a "Murphy's Law" (the original being: "If anything can go wrong, it will.")

In the case of giving up cigarettes, our Murphy's Law reads:

Everything that could possibly go wrong in your life will wait until you're trying to quit smoking before doing so.

In other words: every stressful thing that could possibly happen — things you would normally use cigarettes to soothe the blow of — will wait until you've sworn off cigarettes before knocking on your door!

For example:

Want to get a traffic ticket? Fine: just stop smoking; the cops will be on you like flies on milk, no matter how carefully you drive!

Want to go toe-to-toe with your spouse? No problem: just lay off the cigarettes for an hour or two and the divorce attorneys will be drawing lots to see who gets what!

Had high hopes for that report you wrote at work? Good. Well, keep smoking and your boss will love it; but give **up** smoking and he'll be asking you where you learned Sanskrit and why don't you go back there for a few years to see if you can't learn some more?!

Why this happens — why all these bad things wait until we make a solemn vow to give up smoking before they take turns beating our brains in — is something that only Murphy could answer, and he ain't talking!

We only mention them so you won't be shocked by them when they happen to you.

And if they **don't** happen? Congratulations!

But if they do, don't let them be the reason you start smoking again.

Instead, just ride out Murphy's "storm" and, within days or weeks, you'll be able to tell old Murph exactly what type of flip-top box he can stick his "Law" into!

26
Slip-Slidin' Away

We've already told you that the easiest way to stop smoking is to simply "slip yourself into" the life of a non-smoker. Now we'll tell you the best way to do it:

After you've figured out what a non-smoker does every minute of the day, we want you to actually put yourself into that "picture;" we want you to actually "**see**" yourself

• getting up in the morning and **not** lighting up; instead, see yourself doing everything **else** you would do of a morning — showering, brushing your teeth, combing your hair, etc., but without trying to provide "cover" for the Third Army while you're doing them!

• getting in your car and **not** lighting up; instead: polish the dashboard or pick up lint off the carpet or check your lipstick in the mirror (or your tattooed hand, if Marlboros were your smoke) or stuff some gum in your mouth — **anything** but lighting up a cigarette before you pull out of the driveway!

• finishing breakfast (or your morning coffee break) with an item of food that you **don't** have to set fire to, to enjoy (unless, of course, you just "can't live" without jelly donut *flambé*)

• having lunch with your **non**-smoking friends (You don't have any? Well, brush your teeth and **make** some!)

• sitting at your desk and **not** creating a diorama entitled: "Vesuvius: the Morning After!"

- driving home the same way you drove in, with **all** the air pollution coming "second hand;"
- having dinner and then finding some way to relax **without** drugs, the same way a zillion other people do!
- **reading** yourself to sleep, instead of you-know-what (no, not that; the **other** one!)

Again: we want you to actually see yourself doing all these things — as if you were watching a movie of yourself.

In fact, even better than a movie, why don't you actually **go through the motions** of doing all these things — like, maybe, tomorrow.

Don't stop smoking — Heaven forbid you should do **that**! — just go through the **motions** of a non-smoker, to see what it would feel like if you actually **did** quit!

Of course, if you really **could** get from bed to shower without a cigarette, or from shower to car, or from car to office, or from opening bell to coffee break, or from coffee break to lunch, etc., and if you **could** manage to keep yourself alive for one more day, that would send one message and one message only to your Subconscious: you obviously **didn't** need a cigarette during any of those periods on Monday to make it to Tuesday, so there's really no need for your Subconscious to make you **crave** a cigarette at any of those times on Tuesday, to get you to Wednesday! In other words: You can get there very nicely all by yourself, thank you very much!

And, if you're real lucky, your Subconscious **won't** make you crave a cigarette on Tuesday. And, if you don't **crave** a cigarette, of course, why in God's name would you **smoke** one?!

Again: you eliminate your craving for cigarettes by **consciously** eliminating cigarettes for a day or two or seven — however long it takes your Subconscious to get the message that you don't want to smoke anymore, so that **it** can take over the non-smoking chores **for** you! At which point, it should take a pack of wild horses to get you smoking again!

That's right: just like the one the Marlboro Man rode in on!

27
HOW Many?!

It would be such a comfort if the number of people doing something bore even the faintest resemblance to the "rightness" of doing it. If that **were** the case, then the billions of drinkers would make drinking O. K.; the millions of child-abusers would make child-abuse O. K.; the millions of gallons of crude washing up on California beaches would make oil companies O.K.

You get the picture: If there's one thing that history has shown us, it's that "Fifty million Frenchmen **can** be wrong" — and most often are!

So, before you and your fellow smokers console yourselves, over your next round of Buds, with: "Hey: how bad could smoking be if all of us are doing it?!" ask some surfer how bad **he** thinks it is!

And if you just can't let go of this "safety-in-numbers" lunacy? No problem: I'm sure there's room down there for **all** of you!

Of course, if you look at it in just the right light, "How bad could it be..." really **isn't** that bad an argument!

Oh, not for **smoking**; it's still a loser for that!

Then what else?

Would you believe: **Not** smoking?!

That's right: the same argument you use to stay **on** cigarettes can be used just as easily — and more intelligently — to get **off** them!

How so?

Well, when you use the argument to stay **on** cigarettes, what you're saying is: "How bad could smoking be **physically**, if 'everybody's' doing it? After all, these people can't **all** be suicidal!"

When you use it to get **off** cigarettes, what you're saying is: "How bad could **not** smoking be **psychologically**, if 'everybody's' doing it. After all, these non-smokers aren't **all** nervous wrecks, like **I'd** be if I quit!"

So, strange as it might seem, you can use the same line to go in two completely different directions — and you don't even have to be a politician to do it!

The choice of **which** direction to go in is, of course, completely up to you. All I can do is hope you decide to join the **rest** of us non-basket-cases!

28
Sis-Boom-Bah!

You should come to grips with one thing:

If you're a smoker, every non-smoker in the world is rooting for you to continue your habit.

Why?
Because, compared to someone who doesn't smoke (and all else being equal), someone who does smoke is a "loser" (after all: it's such a dumb, destructive habit, what **other** word could come to mind?!)

So what?
So there are only so many quality jobs, quality spouses, quality schools around; and the more you smoke, the less your chances of landing any of those jobs, spouses, school spots for your children — which, of course, leaves more of them available for **non**-smokers.
So, we ask you: if **you** were a non-smoker, wouldn't **you** be rooting for all the smokers of the world to never change a thing?! Bingo!

Is it unfair that you should be denied so many of life's pleasures because of a silly little habit?
Of course it's unfair! I mean, why should a potential employer think you won't have the intestinal fortitude to see a project through to completion just because you don't have the

guts to take two weeks out of your smoking life to put an end to something that's killing you and everyone around you?! Incredible, isn't it? In fact, the more I think about it, the more I think we've got grounds for a lawsuit here! Let me know how it turns out, would you?!

And those potential lifemates: why **wouldn't** they want to make love to you, and your ashtray mouth, and your nicotine-soaked bed linens, and your still-smoking hair? After all: none of those things makes **you** want to vomit!

Come to think of it: there are so **many** quality people out there who think you're just "**dre-e-e-eamy**," surrounded by a cloud of smoke all day, why should you waste your time with some stuck-up prude who doesn't?!

And we hear you: what's wrong with **public** school?! It was good enough for **you**, wasn't it?! O. K.: so it was more like **reform** school, with just a tiny bit of teaching thrown in, so they could keep their funding. But it got you where you are today, didn't it? So how bad could it have been?!

You know, you're right: there are still so many glorious things waiting out there for people who smoke, you'd have to be an **idiot** to quit!   Forget we even mentioned it!

Of course, there's one thing you should **never** forget:

You're only here once.

If you want to spend that "once" as a smoker, no one's going to stop you.

In fact, no one **can** stop you: only **you** can call a halt to your addiction.

Do you **have** to call a halt to it?

Of course not:

As long as the thought of sudden death from a heart attack or the lingering death of cancer doesn't bother you, it certainly won't bother **me**! Might bother the family that depends on you for its livelihood, but that's why we've made finding **new** spouses so easy!

Of course, since it's never been **proven** that smoking causes heart attacks or lung cancer, we might be stretching things by saying that smoking **kills** you!

In fact, when you think about it: if smoking **did** kill you, smokers would be dropping like flies, every time they lit up! Since they're not — at least **I've** never seen any — maybe we should go a little easier on this "smoking **kills** you" routine.

In fact, it would probably be better if we came up with a new word altogether for getting dead from smoking, since "kill" is definitely too strong.

How about..."stupid?"

30
Renoir

The main reason you smoke, of course, is to impress every-one with your "coolness," your "worldliness," your "sophistica-tion."

Mm-hm.

Want to know just how much of an impression you're making? Well, try **not** smoking for a week or a year and see how many people notice that you've quit.

That's O.K., we'll save you the trouble: no one will notice.

So what?

So, if nobody notices that you've quit, just how much of an impression do you think you were making on them when you **hadn't**?!

What's that?: You don't care how impressed everybody **else** is with your "talents" as long as you keep "snowing" that guy in the mirror?!

Ooh — sorry. Our mistake.

31
Enjoy!

But I **enjoy** smoking!"

Right. And Heinrich Himmler enjoyed throwing Jews and Gypsies into gas chambers. So that's some great recommendation for doing something: "I **enjoy** it!"

Do us a favor: You want to enjoy something? Then find something **else** to enjoy — something that doesn't make the cigarette companies so rich it takes half the Gross National Product of the Western World to buy one!

"...I enjoy it............"
Give me a break!

32
Adiós Amigos!

Those of you who are **not** smoking to kill yourself can skip this chapter; for the rest of you, who view smoking as the easiest way out of your worst nightmare — life — we'd like to talk to you for a minute:

First of all, you're right: life **is** a nightmare:
- parents who brought you up badly or not at all;
- people trying to cheat you, every time you turn around;
- a job that demeans you and doesn't care if it uses even a **tenth** of your ability;
- industrialists competing with each other to see who can choke you to death, or water-pollute you to death, or acid-rain you to death first;
- bankers who line up to give swindlers billions, but won't lend hard-working **you** a **dime**!;
- schools where it was more important to **toe** the line than to **learn** very many;
- governments that take, take, take and give back nothing in return, except for maybe cluster bombs and Three-Mile Islands — while our schools, highways, hospitals and farms all fight with one another for top spot on the Extinct Species list!

Yes, life is a nightmare.

Only one question, though: if you're trying to **leave** that nightmare, why are you taking such a long time to do it! I mean, you talk to a soldier who's about to go on what is most likely a suicide mission and he'll tell you one thing and one thing only:

"I hope I get it quick: a round to the head or one through the heart. The **last** thing I want is a lingering death!" (as if you could order up the way you die!)

So, I ask you again: Since everyone else who wants to commit suicide wants it to happen as **quickly** as possible, why is it that you don't mind it taking 40 or 50 years?! If life is really that bad, why are you taking a half-century to **leave** it?!

And if the last thing your average suicide wants is a lingering — and painful — death, why is that exactly what you — Mr. or Mrs. Cigarette Suicide — are shooting for?! Or don't you **know** what it's like to slowly "drown" from emphysema while you sit in your rocker, surrounded by an **ocean** of air?! Or to have every nerve in your body pumping out unbearable pain, day after day after day, as a cancer goes through you the way Sherman went through Georgia?!

You **don't** know what those are like? Then maybe you should get down to your nearest cancer ward or emphysema ward, watch the way people are dying there and **then** make up your mind if that's really the way you want to go!

Are we saying that you should commit suicide **faster**?! Of course not: for every botched government program, there's a clear, cold mountain stream somewhere, just waiting for you to escape to it; for every demolished highway, there's a spectacular new mall going up somewhere, filled with hundreds of dazzling shops selling millions of glorious goodies that very few dead people will ever be lining up for; for every bad parent, there are loads of new friends out there, just waiting for you to take the time and trouble to find them!

No, we're not telling you to commit suicide — fast **or** slow! All we're saying is: as long as you're not committing suicide the way **suicides** commit suicide, why bother doing it at all?!

Instead of devoting 50 years to checking **out** of life, why not use the same half-century to check life **out**; to see all the **good** things life has to offer and maybe even **add** to those good things by turning some of the bad ones around! You can, you know, but not if you're lost to the world in a cloud of smoke!

So, is "suicide" an "answer?"
Of **course** it's an "answer!" It's **always** an "answer!"

Then what's the "question?"
Just as obvious:

"What's the absolute dumbest thing a human being can do with his life?"

If that concept sits well with you — doing the dumbest thing with your life you can possibly do — then by all means keep on doing it!; keep committing suicide in the slowest way you know how.

But if it ever starts to bother you — that the jerk the next table over is **not** doing the dumbest thing with his life that he possibly can, even though he's never done anything **else** right — then you might consider coming in off your "ledge," taking the elevator down to the ground floor and starting to treat your life like the gift that it is — and one, as it happens, you'll never get again!

If you do make that decision, we and about a billion of your closest friends and relatives will be waiting for you, down at the door.

We can't, of course, wait forever.

Can you?

33
Luck and Pluck

It's hard to quit smoking; it's hard to give up **any** drug, break **any** habit.

Is that a good reason to **keep** smoking?

"Yes," for an awful lot of you: much easier to simply give in to the urge on Monday and then pray like a banshee on Tuesday that all the things that are killing every other smoker in the world will somehow lose your address!

And if they don't?

"Oh well: 'luck of the draw,' I guess."

Care to guess how many smokers **lose** their draw every year, for no reason at all?

Not that we have anything against luck and prayer: we've never turned our back on either one of them and have no immediate plans to! It's just that, like everything else in life: no matter how good something is all by itself, it can only get better with a little bit of help:

As good as a pair of boots might be, there's still no better way to stay dry in Winter than to never see snow in the first place;

No matter how good your car's bumper might be, who would choose **it** to save your life if "never hitting anything" was the other choice?

So, while we're not **downgrading** the role luck and prayer play in warding off disease, all we're asking is: how much **worse** off could you be, **helping** that luck and prayer by ridding yourself of what maybe 10 or 15 people worldwide sincerely believe is **causing** those diseases?

So, please don't think we're saying you won't be the lucky one whose prayers will be answered; after all, **someone** has to win the Lottery (yes, we know: not every week and, now that we think of it, not all that often. Still, on those rare occasions when someone **does** win.......).

All we're saying is: how much harm could it do, to **help** those prayers? After all, wouldn't the Lottery get a mite easier if you already had five of the six numbers?!

So, don't stop praying and for God's sake don't lose your lucky rabbit's foot (though it's questionable how much luck it brought the rabbit!) Both are simply **smashing** ways to keep from getting sick (they must be, since they're all you're relying on to do it for you).

It's just that I'm sure neither of them would be offended if you didn't rely **exclusively** on them to get you through the minefield of smoking-related diseases, the way John Wayne did. Or Bette Davis. Or Humphrey Bogart. Or Yul Brynner. Or Robert Taylor. Or Gary Cooper. Or Harry Reasoner. Or.................

34
The Gordian Knot

A lot of people resist the temptation to quit smoking because they're afraid of the weight gain that always seems to go with it.

We'd like to tell you that you'll be the one in a million who **won't** gain weight, but, in all candor, you'd be better off playing the Lottery.

So, since "everyone" who quits smoking gains weight, the question becomes: Why?

The answer?

For a lot of reasons:

1) You stop poisoning your mouth, so food **tastes** better;

2) You stop poisoning your system, so food gets **absorbed** better;

3) All smokers are "oral" anyway, which means you have to have **something** going on around your mouth all the time. And if it's not "cigarettes".... "Hey: where'd you stick that five-pound bag of Famous Amos??!"

4) Certain types and certain quantities of food can have almost as sedating an effect on you as nicotine; since you're addicted to the sedation as much as to the cigarettes.....

5) As an "addictive personality," you have to maintain a certain **level** of addiction at all times, and when smoking is no longer doing **its** part to maintain that level, the slack has to be taken up by anything **else** you might be addicted to: eating; drinking; and whatever else might be holding a higher-calorie ticket than the addiction you're now "eighty-sixing."

Whatever the reason(s), the facts remain the same: "quit smoking and you'll gain weight." So you don't, so you won't.

No problem there, except that we're not talking about staying with crocheting here; we're talking about not giving up a **deadly habit** simply because you don't want to trade one "killer" for another — especially for one that makes you look and feel so bad!

Fair enough!

But where does it say the only way to stay thin — or to **get** thin, if you've been feeding yourself more than Marlboros these last few decades — is by controlling what you eat?

In fact, and at the risk of sounding self-serving, there's something spreading across this continent (and several other continents at last report) called the Walk Yourself Thin Program, that has all but "pink-slipped" eating-control programs (what you would call "diets") as the method of choice for getting thin and/or staying thin.

What does this mean?

It means that it doesn't matter how much your food intake increases when you quit smoking; as long as you have a Thinwalking program already in place, you can simply **walk off** all those extra calories, at least until your body stops "celebrating" the fact that it's not being poisoned 40 or 60 times a day!

And **will** you have a Thinwalking program "already in place?" Well, you should — but not for the purposes of walking yourself thin:

The fact is: the best way to stay off cigarettes is to remind yourself, at least once a day, of the physical damage you'd be doing to yourself if you went back on the smokes. And the best way to do that is by doing some sort of reasonably-vigorous exercise — strenuous enough, at least, to get your lungs working — every day.

Earlier on, we recommended "brisk walking" as that exercise, since it's an exercise that's as good as any and, what's more, is one that you should easily be able to do every day (unlike water skiing, swimming, aerobic dancing, etc., that require special equipment or special training or a special setting).

So, if you have a "walking-to-stay-off-cigarettes" program already in place, I certainly won't tell anyone if you make each of those steps do "double duty:" not just walking to stay off cigarettes, but walking to stay thin (or get thin) as well!

And if you **don't** have such a program already in place? What are you waiting for?!

35
Thanks for the Memories!

If you **are** going to quit smoking, of course, you're going to have to come to a decision (not easy for someone who hands his decision-making powers over to a pack of rolled-up plants a hundred times a day): you've got to decide who's going to control your life from here on out — you or Philip Morris.

Of course, there's nothing really wrong with putting yourself in Philip Morris's hands every day — or R. J. Reynolds's; or P. Lorillard's; or Liggett & Myers's. After all, they've taken pretty good care of you so far — given you back all the things that smoking their products has taken away from you: your health today; your health tomorrow; your feeling of **real** self-respect (yes: you "respect" your ability to take searing-hot smoke into your lungs without doubling over, but that's something else).

In fact, now that we think of it, the tobacco companies have taken **such** good care of you so far that you're an absolute **pig** if you haven't already **thanked** them for doing so. Luckily, this oversight is easily corrected: all it takes is a card or letter — which you can send to any and all of your favorites:

Philip Morris
Richmond, VA 23261

R. J. Reynolds
Winston-Salem, NC 27102

Liggett & Myers
Durham, NC 27702

P. Lorillard
Greensboro, NC 27420

The American Tobacco Co.
Reidsville, NC 27320

Brown & Williamson
Louisville, KY 40232

Benson & Hedges
Richmond, VA 23261

And what should you say to these wonderful people, these friends of yours who've singlehandedly and singlemindedly made up for all the bad things their products have done to you and will continue to do if you don't stop them?

Well, we can tell you what **not** to say:

You remember when the oil companies were ripping everybody off, back in the mid-70's (they called it "windfall profits" then, but we all knew what they were talking about).

You remember who they hired, to help them counteract all the bad press their out-and-out thievery had been bringing them? That's right: the American Flag-with-Legs: Bob Hope!

And what was his message; how did old Ski Nose calm our gas-lines furor?

By reminding us that the oil companies weren't owned by some hideous robber barons, sitting in million-dollar penthouses somewhere, trying to figure out even more **devious** ways to squeeze an extra 300% or 400% profit out of every drop of oil—

("Let's see: why don't we tell the bozos that....OK — I've got it: 'The Arabs have stopped shipping us oil and there's no way we can make up the shortfall in less than...' — how long did you say it would take for the price of gasoline to double?")

("Uh, let's see" [shuffling of papers] "—'Four months,' sir")

("'...Four months — but that we're doing everything

humanly possible in the meantime to keep prices as low as we
reasonably can.' How does that sound?")

("Sounds great, J. B.!")

([SOUND OF LAUGHTER IN LARGE OFFICE, FOL-
LOWED BY SOUNDS OF ROUSING TOAST]).

Oh no, Bob told us, the oil companies weren't owned by
robber barons; the oil companies were owned by little grand-
mothers, rocking on porches out in East Jesus, Missouri, somewhere, and by every Cub Scout and Brownie you ever knew —
all of whom would starve to death in minutes if anyone dared
threaten their only source of income: those poor little oil companies!

I don't know about you, but I, for one, thanked God right
then and there that Bob had set us straight:

The oil companies are **not** owned by robber barons.
They're **run** by robber barons, of course, but hey: how much can
you jam into a minute's commercial when you've got so many
grandmas and Cub Scouts to push onstage?

Why bring this up here?

To remind you that the big tobacco companies are no
different than the big oil companies: each is owned by a lot of
grandmas and Cub Scouts, and by a lot of pension funds that will
be the sole source of income for millions of factory workers and
tens of millions of government employees when they retire —
provided there's anything left in them after they've been so
creatively managed by their well-meaning and completely-in-
corruptible administrators.

So what?

So, we don't want you going off half-cocked — after you
wake up to what the tobacco companies have **really** been doing
to your life — and endangering all these poor people's livelihoods with threats to "expose" those companies and to sue them
for "every nickel they've got" (which would, of course, do you no
good anyway, since no tobacco company representative ever put
a gun to your head to use his organization's products; threw lots
of **advertising** your way that made you feel like a Commie
retard if you **didn't** use them, but no "guns," as we know them.)

Instead, take whatever time you need to, to calm yourself

down; and then, instead of **railing** at these companies, tell them how **proud** you are to be giving up the only lungs you'll ever have so a little old grandma out in East Jesus could rock herself to sleep at night — even if it means that **you'll** be rocking yourself to sleep just east of Jesus a lot sooner than you ever thought you would — or needed to!

Depending on how much you smoke, I wouldn't wait real **long** to thank them. In fact, why don't you do it right now, so you'll have time to read the super-nice letter they'll be sending back to you, right after they've finished yours?
Or you.

36
"That's a Wrap!"

So, your choice is simple:

Keep thinking that smoking, which is killing millions, won't kill you;

That lung cancer, which hunts down millions of smokers every year, will never find you;

That the pain you get in your chest, every time you light up, might be due to a million things — heat, cold, pollution, humidity, dryness — but never to that cigarette you're smoking;

That you "haven't lost a step" because of your habit — physically **or** mentally;

That smoking really **is** an incredibly-sophisticated activity, and that the whole world is absolutely in awe of you for doing it;

That all cigarettes are is a cheap sedative — and a less dangerous one at that than "hard" drugs like Librium and Valium. And, since you can't make it through your hectic day without **some** kind of sedation, better to do it with cigarettes than with something you need a **doctor's** degree to get;

That your skin doesn't really look that bad — doesn't look that much different, in fact, than everybody else's your age — and, if it **does** show signs of premature wear, that could be due to a lot of things — acid rain, the threat of war, heat, cold, dryness, humidity — but almost certainly **not** to the artery-squeezing, cell-starving effects of nicotine;

That **everybody** coughs all the time;

That people should worry more about their children's table manners than about how much second-hand smoke is blowing their way, smoke that doesn't kill any more people each year than **car** accidents do;

That if smoking were really such a dangerous habit, why would millions of people still be doing it?!

Or you can wake up, realize that the wonderful effects you're getting from your drug addiction are **not** coming without a price, and tell the world, and the American Tobacco Company, that you're no longer willing to **pay** that price for a habit you somehow lived happily without for the first decade or two of your life!

That's it; that's your choice.

And it really is **your** choice: no one else can make it for you.

All we out here can do is tell you what happened to us the day **we** quit — which, looking back on it, was the happiest day of our lives (though at the time, of course, the word "happy" was probably the furthest one from our lips!)

Are we now, eight years later, free of all desire for the drug?

Ha!:

The day does not go by that we don't consider lighting up again!

Then why don't we?

For a lot of reasons:

1) Horror at the thought of enriching some good ol' companies and their good ol' advertising agencies;

2) The hideous cost of cigarettes (three bucks a day is over a thousand dollars a year!);

3) The ability to take a deep breath without looking around, halfway through it, to see who's shoved a knife between our ribs;

4) The fact that we can now get as much oxygen as we need to, to walk fast or run semi-fast;

5) The reminder that millions of people are crying them-selves to sleep every night because they **can't** kick the habit, and there we are, finally free of it for some lucky reason, and all we can think about is going back on it?! Give me a break!

When we "balance" all of the above against the "privi-lege" of once again getting nicotinely-numb, the scales always tip in favor of staying "clean."

And that's where they stay tipped.

Until the next day.

When the nightmare starts all over again:

"Was smoking really that bad? Did it really take away that much of my lung capacity? Couldn't I start smoking again and still walk or run as fast as I wanted to?

"And not everyone gets lung cancer or stomach cancer or colon cancer or bladder cancer or emphysema or heart attacks or strokes from smoking.

"I mean, how bad could it be if so many are still doing it? Those people couldn't all be dumb! There are a lot of smokers who have good heads on their shoulders. Couldn't they know what they're doing?

"And that taste! Now that I've been off them for so many years, I'll bet those little guys would taste as good as they did the first time I tried one.

"And God knows, I could use the calming effect that cigarettes can give me."

Well, we could all use a calming effect;

And I hear that even cyanide tastes good to some — though not on what you would call a continuing basis.

And 50 million Frenchmen can be wrong.

And you're right: not every smoker gets all of those deadly diseases. But every smoker is right at the top of the list to get at least one of them, and how many more would it take?!

And the smoke from a burning plant can rob you of over 90% of your breathing capacity — though, of course, that might be considered "not much" by some people — certainly by those guys over at the "Institute."

And that's the nightmare every ex-smoker goes through every day — the constant fight over whether or not to start up again. Which tells you how strong the drug is, and how strong the drug's advertising is.

And what is the end result of this "nightmare?" The appreciation that, with all the "good" things about smoking, you've still found a way to stay clear of it for one more day, which has made your lungs one day cleaner, your heart one day stronger, your skin one day younger, your clothes, hair, car one day sweeter, your life one day better.

The main thing your victory gives you, though, is the grateful feeling, when you watch someone else lighting up, of: "There but by the grace of God go I."

Do those smokers enjoy what they're doing?
Of course they do!
Would you enjoy it?
Of course you would!
Why do you think they call it a "drug?!"

Could they enjoy not doing it? Could you?!
Of course!

Just remember: you most likely spent the first 10 to 20 years of your life without lighting up and you apparently lived to tell about it, so there's nothing "natural" about smoking, nothing about it you need to do, to make it from one day to the next.

Which means you can wake yourself up from a living nightmare, can convince yourself that you've gotten yourself into a hole that has no bottom, whose only real promise is for a permanent indentation in the Earth's surface!

If you can do that, admit that, the battle is more than half won. If you can't, maybe you know someone who can, someone who would like to stay around a bit longer than Philip Morris thinks he or she should. If you do know someone like that, feel free to pass this little book along to him or her.

Why?

Of course: So this book can do for them what it could have done for you!

37
Postscript

Following is the text of a TV announcement that actor/ director Yul Brynner prepared just before his death from metastatic lung cancer:

By the time you see this, I will be dead.

Yes, you are looking at my image and hearing my voice, so I seem to be alive. But it's all an illusion.

Don't believe me? Then try writing me a letter and see what sort of reply you get.

I didn't want to die; I really enjoyed living — at least as much as I hope you enjoyed my work in The King and I, Westworld, The Magnificent Seven and a long list of other movie and TV projects I either starred in or helped bring to life.

And yet, with all my wanting to live, I am now as dead as the television set you're watching me on.

No more will I smell the first fresh breaths of Spring; never again hear children laughing, as they dream the dreams that can't come true, but sometimes do, because they dream them; no more feel the smooth, soft skin of my life's true love.

All that was good about life has been taken from me; all that I or anyone would want to experience forever I will experience no more.

And why?

Because a hundred cigarettes a day were more important to me than all the wives and children and Springtimes in Creation;

Because I was too stupid to admit that what I was doing could kill me — as if the cells inside me knew that I never wanted to die and would respect my wishes by never turning against me and eating me alive;

Because I thought I needed those cigarettes to keep my creative juices flowing — conveniently overlooking the fact that some of the most creative minds ever born never needed a drop of poison, to walk off with all the prizes;

Because I was too weak to do without this "harmless pleasure" for the day or two it would have taken me to find a really harmless one!

And because of all that, I am now dead.

Would I have lived forever? Of course not. But when they've all been taken from you, a single day becomes "forever!"

And what would I give for that one more day — especially if that day were free of all the pain and misery my stupid habit cost me? Hmph: how much time do you have?!

Do I want to see you go away with me, so we can swap smoking yarns with one another? Yes — if it will put an end to your pain the way it put an end to mine.

And do I want such pain for you if you don't already have it?

Well, why do you think I'm talking to you now?

So, I'm dead — as dead as you'll be if you don't take control of your life back from whoever owns it.

Is it hard to quit?
Of course it's hard.
But you want "hard?" Try asking me over for dinner!

As for me — I'd better save my breath, since I have so little left; I should have had a lot more, but I gave the rest of it away.

My only hope is that I gave mine away so you wouldn't have to — a little like that carpenter fellow from Nazareth did, a long, long time ago. If that is the case, I can go to my rest with a little more peace. If it's not — if you can't wait to follow me down to wherever I'm going — then I will have died in vain — and so will you!

End of Transmission

Glossary

Abandonment: Empty feeling you get right after a loved one dies or you quit smoking.

Acid Rain: Every-day-is-Christmas gift from industrial giants to political midgets; not as bad an environmental problem as originally thought — especially for those it doesn't fall on.

Actions: The way you "talk" to your Subconscious Mind and "tell" it where you want it to take you: abuse yourself and your Subconscious will abuse you; **stop** abusing yourself and your Subconscious will have no reason to (See also: **Laws of Nature**).

Addict: Someone having the time of his life, no matter what that **does** to his "time" (see also: **Dead-end Street**).

Addiction, Physical: "Impossible to get from cigarettes" (common knowledge in the 1940's and '50's); therefore: main reason smokers felt confident about taking the cigarette plunge way back then; also: main reason smokers **keep** taking the plunge — 40 or 60 times a day, day after day after day....................

Addictions (all): What every other nation would love you to believe is a dynamite base to build a Great Society on.

Addictive Personality: Someone who "can't wait" to turn his life over to everything else.

Address: Where everything can find you, sooner or later.

Advertising: A pleasant lubricant, used to grease the wheels of change.

Advertising Agency: Group of otherwise normal people who grow rabid when it comes time to sell their clients' product(s); also: only source of consistently-creative entertainment in the last decades of the 20th century.

Aerobic Dancing: Exercise dreamed up by joint specialist while awaiting the birth of his fourth child.

Agony: Feeling of pain, relieved by rooting out the causes or by sugar-coating them (see also: **Cigarettes; Booze; Heroin;...........**)

Aimless Drifting: Non-directed behavior, typical of icebergs on the ocean and people without goals.

Air: "Nothing special" to a non-smoker; distant memory to an emphysemic.

Air Pollution: First-hand: What **you** create;

Second-hand: What the rest of the world thinks you just can't live without.

Albeit (pronounced "all-be-it"): Fancy way of saying "although" that every writer is entitled to use at least **once** in his lifetime!

"Alive with Pleasure:" Advertising slogan of Newport Cigarettes (product of P. Lorillard Co.) in the 1980's and '90's; some question as to amount of consultation done by Lorillard staff with cancer specialists, emphysema specialists, heart specialists and undertakers before use of the word "alive" with **anything** related to cigarettes

American Tobacco Company, the: One of seven companies in the mid-South (*which see*) dedicated to preserving the physical and mental well-being of the American people — thus the logical and totally-inoffensive taking of this country's great name as part of its own.

American Tobacco Institute: Group of otherwise-nice folks, working their hardest to prove that inhaling one of the deadliest poisons known to man — nicotine — and a substance that causes cancer in everything **else** it touches — "tar" — is, in fact, of no particular danger to human tissue; also: Club Med for the Tooth Fairy and Santa Claus (*which see*).

Annual Report: What corporations use, to tell the world how well they seem to be doing and how well they'll **definitely** be doing in the coming years; those produced by tobacco companies are real, real thick.

Anxiety: Bad feeling you get, that all is "not right;" relieved by meticulously finding out **why** all is not right and then making it so, or by getting doped out of your skull.

Arabs: Group of highly-intelligent people who stopped fighting among themselves long enough to conquer most of the known world between the 8th and 15th Centuries, before picking up again right where they left off.

Area Code: Several-square-mile area where all telephones have the same three-digit calling code; also: as close to a Lottery booth as a poor person (and a lot of rich ones) should ever get.

Ashtray (Car): Ideally: something that should be as clean when your car goes into a museum as it was the day you bought it; also: the apparent reason smokers smash their cars up at a rate four times that of non-smokers, as they look to find it in the dark.

Ashtray Facial: The only way a smoker can smell what every non-smoker has been smelling from Mars (*which see*).

"Ashtray Mouth:" To a smoker: oral-shaped structure with four slots cut in it; To a non-smoker: hopefully not what Coco had in mind for her fall fragrance collection.

Asteroid: Enormous chunk of rock, hurtling along in outer space — best kept right there (see also: **Cigarettes**).

Astronauts: Until recently: latter-day reminders of what King Arthur must have had going; currently: highly-trained collectors of unemployment checks.

Athlete's Foot: Irritation and cracking of skin between toes, caused by a fungus; rumored to be under investigation by the American Tobacco Institute as the Number One Cause of Preventable Death in the Known Universe (see also: **Scurvy; Beri-beri; Cold Sores**).

Autofocus Cameras: Japan's reminder to the rest of the world that she can **always** be smarter than you are, anytime she wants!

Awe: Feeling of amazement, wonder, respect, etc., that every smoker is sure everyone in the civilized world is feeling toward him, due to his incredible ability to set fire to a plant.

Ax-murderer: Someone as apparently proud of his or her career as you are of yours.

Banshee: In Irish and Scottish folklore: a supernatural being, taking the shape of an old woman and foretelling death by mournful singing or wailing outside a dwelling; model for smokers trying to keep death **from** their door.

Barleycorn, John: Slang name for booze; visits many more homes each night than even the Tooth Fairy (*which see*).

Barrier (to Quitting): The drug addiction you can't possibly get from cigarettes.

Base Pipe: Rocket of choice for freebase cocaine addicts on the expressway to Heaven.

Basket: Final resting place for anything that becomes permanently unglued; where smokers imagine they'll wind up if they stop doping themselves to death.

Bedroom: Place where you first do most of your "special things" — not always (thank God) alone.

Beechcraft Corporation: Manufacturer of small, expensive planes, where you fly all cramped up (see also: **Boeing Corporation**).

Beer Commercial: Prime function: To let you know the way life should **really** be lived. And if you're **not** living it that way? What's the matter: You can't find a liquor store?!

Beri-beri: Disease due to deficiency of Vitamin B_1, now seen mainly in Mongolia; under investigation by American Tobacco Institute as possibly being the Number One Cause of Preventable Death in the Known Universe.

Bias: Prejudicial feelings that non-smokers exhibit toward smokers, apparently for no (cough) good (cough) reason.

Bic: Disposable butane lighter, used to ignite disposable cigarettes, for the purpose of getting smoke into apparently disposable lungs.

Big Board, the: The New York Stock Exchange, where up-to-the-minute share prices used to be posted on a large blackboard; also: tobacco companies' best friend.

Big Oil Companies: Large organizations that make hideous amounts of money by sucking up a lot of black, tarry stuff that's been buried in the Earth for a long, long time (see also: **Big Tobacco Companies**).

Big Tobacco Companies: Large organizations that make hideous amounts of money with a product that requires its user to suck in a lot of black, tarry stuff that stays buried in his lungs for a long, long time (see also: **Big Oil Companies**).

Billions: Number of people who don't smoke and don't miss it; also: approximate number of dollars in average tobacco company's petty cash drawer.

Biopsy: Removal of a piece of tissue from a living organism, to test for presence of disease — most often cancer.

Birthright: Something that's your **due**; something that's **owed** to you merely because you showed up (see also: **Civil Service**).

Black and White: What everyone would like the world to be, but what it never is (see also: **Free**).

Black Tie Party: Elegant affair where tobacco companies have hard evidence that rich people spend all their time smoking, which is how those people got rich and how they stay that way (see also: **Necktie Party**).

Boca Raton: City in South Florida, whose name translates to: "The Mouse's Mouth;" need help establishing connection between million-dollar mansions and potentially-rabid, small rodent orifice.

Boeing Corporation: Manufacturer of large, expensive planes where you fly all cramped up (see also: **Beechcraft Corporation**).

Bogart, Humphrey: Tough-guy star of *Casablanca, The African Queen, The Caine Mutiny* and a host of other films he acted and smoked his way through; long dead of throat and lung cancer.

Bogie: Humphrey Bogart's nickname (*which see*).

Bogey: Best score a smoker can ever hope to attain in the golf game of life.

***Bonnie and Clyde* :** Marvelous 1968 film detailing the lives and careers of Depression-era bank robbers Bonnie Parker, who enjoyed smoking cigars, and Clyde Barrow, who, legend has it, was hard-pressed to smoke **anything**!

Boredom: What smokers "defeat" a hundred times a day with just a flick of their Bic (*which see*).

Booze: Slang name for alcohol you drink, to distinguish it from the alcohol you use to preserve tissue specimens.

"Bottom Line:" In general: the end result of all that precedes it; in smokers: usually found about six feet below the **top** line.

Bozo: Name of a hopelessly-inept clown who believes everything everyone tells him.

Brain: Highly-moldable body part that doesn't require an anvil, to get beaten into shape: the silk from an advertiser's purse is quite strong enough to do the job.

Breakfast: traditionally: the first meal of the day; usually falls somewhere between an average smoker's 10th and 11th cigarettes.

Breathing Deeply: Main pastime of ex-smokers; something to be studiously avoided by those still coming "Alive with Pleasure" every day (*which see*).

Bricks: Rock-hard rectangles, used for building fortresses to keep undesirable things out but often just as effective at keeping them in, depending on who made the bricks.

Bridge: Highly-addictive card game, invented by the World Tobacco Cartel.

Broker: Someone who makes a living by convincing you that he alone knows the best path between where your money is and where it ought to be — which has to make you wonder why he's still **working** for a living.

Brownie: Female equivalent of Cub Scout (*which see*).

Brynner, Yul: Late actor/director (*The King and I, Westworld, The Magnificent Seven*), who admitted to smoking five packs of cigarettes a day — until, one day, he stopped...for a long, long time.

"Bud:" Shortened form of "Budweiser" — reputed to be the "King of Beers," though some question as to impartiality of coronation committee.

Busybodies: People who spend so much time in smokers' hair they don't have any left over to comb their own!

Butane Conservation Program: What every "chain smoker" is majoring in.

Caesar, Julius: Roman leader, done in by his buddies in the Senate; later praised by one of his former lieutenants, who not only demanded retribution for the leader's ouster, but then proceeded to set up a government of his own (see also: **Gorbachev, M. S.; Yeltsin, B. N.**).

"Calming:" The effect that artery-squeezing, cell-starving nicotine has on your brain; also: the effect running it over would have on your cat.

Camel: Thoroughly-disagreeable animal, recently transformed into thoroughly-suave, thoroughly-**lovable** animal through the magic of Ostrichvision.

Cancer: Fairly serious disease in which previously-normal cells begin multiplying out of control and spreading themselves all over Creation, destroying life-giving tissue in the process (see also: **Big Tobacco Companies**).

Cancer Ward: Where shares in the One More Chance Corporation do real well.

Cancerous Coal: Something burning, ideally, in someone else's furnace.

Candy (Hard): God's gift to people trying to get off cigarettes.

"Can't Stand Up:" Marker signaling endpoint of every alcohol/brain titration (*which see*).

Capone, Al: Reputedly brutal Chicago-area gangster, finally jailed for not paying his taxes, thereby threatening the livelihoods of weapons manufacturers, tobacco growers, government pension fund managers, third-generation welfare families, etc.

Carpenter Fellow (from Nazareth): Jesus Christ.

Carboxymethylcellulose: "Active ingredient" in cigarette filters; made up of a handful of carboxy's, a whole mess of methyl's and more cellulose than you can shake a stick at. Only filters out about 1% of the harmful stuff in cigarette smoke, but does a beautiful job on that 1%.

Carton: Convenient way of getting **ten** packs of cigarettes into youngsters' hands instead of just one, thereby saving them a lot of back-breaking trips to the liquor store.

Cartwheels: Expressions of joy.

Cash Register: Mechanical or electronic device used for registering sales and storing the day's receipts. The one owned by the American Tobacco Company is rumored to have a family of four living in the "Dimes" slot, while they wait for their new condo to be finished.

Change: Something that everybody hates but everybody embraces, the minute everybody else does.

Chapel: Room inside a house of worship where you rarely can smoke.

Cheroots: A cute name for cigars; and the cuter they get, the more harmless they seem.

Chest: Area of your body, easy to puff out: temporarily, with pride; permanently, with emphysema.

Chest Pains: Caused by a lot of things, but "cigarettes isn't one of them" (American Tobacco Institute Study, soon to be released); (see also: **Pollen; Oil Crises; Kids' Recitals; etc.**)

Child Abuse: What everyone else is doing to his children.

Chiclets: Popular, candy-coated chewing gum squares, sold in a long, flat box; much better looking in a shirt pocket than a pack of cigarettes; just ask your kids.

Children: Small individuals who can ruin your day but "make" your lifetime.

Chivas: Short for "Chivas Regal:" extremely-good Scotch Whiskey that allows drunks to drive over small children with approximately the same frequency as extremely-**bad** Scotch Whiskey.

Christening: Religious ritual, where newborn child is welcomed into the House of God; also: social ritual where smokers welcome each other into the new house they bought.

Chumminess: Delightful feeling of camaraderie felt between you and your cigarettes; therefore, one of the 26 main reasons why it's so hard to quit the habit; also: delightful feeling of camaraderie felt between cigarette manufacturers, cigarette wholesalers, cigarette retailers and an awful lot of Mercedes-Benz dealers.

Chummy: The type of habit smoking is, until chips suddenly start getting cashed in while the game is still very much alive.

Christmas: Delightful time of year when people show how much they care about their smoking, drinking friends by giving them gaily-wrapped packages of cigarettes and booze.

Cigarette: Ironically enough: name of a very fast boat, favored by people whose life's goal is to spread drugs throughout America; also: delightful-smelling, tobacco-filled paper tube, of no particular social import in its unlit state.

Cigarette Advertising: Formerly: main source of revenue for TV and radio stations; outlawed in early 1970's, in attempt to reduce its pervasive influence. Currently: main source of revenue for magazine publishers; billboard owners; auto race impresarios; auto race drivers; tennis tournaments; movie producers; rodeos;...............

Cigars: Delicious tobacco creations that **everybody** would smoke, if they didn't smell so bad; so smokers content themselves with cigarettes, which, of course, have no smell at all.

Cirrhosis (liver): Where delicate liver tissue finally learns what it would have been like to be born as rawhide (see also: **Emphysema**).

Civil Engineers: Historically: Boring individuals, directly responsible for building cities up (see also: **Tobacco Company Executives**).

Claymore: Type of land mine (see also: **Minefield**).

Clear Lungs: Everyone's birthright, except victims of cystic fibrosis and Benson & Hedges.

Clothing: Final resting place for all the nicotine and tar that manages to escape the greedy clutches of a smoker's lungs (see also: **Hair; Furniture; Dog; Drapes; Car; Office; Goldfish; Children;...........**)

Cluster Bombs: Really nifty way of blowing up lots of different things all at once; what the United States is apparently banking on, to educate its children.

Cocaine: Drug presumed to be purely "recreational" prior to the 1980's, at which point someone discovered that you could convert it to a smokable form, at which point it became about as "recreational" as World War II — especially among the poorer members of society and those looking to **become** poor.

Coffee: Beverage invented by the World Tobacco Cartel to mask the effect their own product has on non-replaceable brain cells.

Coffee Break: Time period invented by trade unions, for the purpose of allowing smokers to gather together in one spot, to compare notes on the marvelousness and complete safety of their life's love.

Coffin: The original flip-top box, in use long before Marlboro's version was so much as a glint in some origami freak's eye (see also [what else?]: **Origami**).

Cold Sores: Nuisance skin eruptions, usually in the area of the mouth, caused by a Herpes virus; rumored to be under investigation by the American Tobacco Institute as the Number One Cause of Preventable Death in the Known Universe.

College: Place where you learn lots of things — especially, if you're a smoker, where the campus representatives for all the tobacco companies live.

Coma: A state of consciousness somewhere between life and death, and usually far more costly to maintain than either.

Commie: Short for "Communist:" someone who thinks that Communism is just a peachy-keen way to run a country (see also: **Extinct Species List**).

"Con Job:" Short for "confidence job:" usually characterized by opening statement: "You can trust me; I won't hurt you;" constant concern of the world's tobacco companies in their never-ending struggle to protect John Q. Public from the underhanded tactics of anti-smoking crusaders.

Connoisseur: Appreciation for the finer things in life, obtained either by a lifetime of experience or by lighting up after junior high school (see also: **Sophistication**).

"Cons" (as in "Pros and Cons"): Reasons for not doing something; average smoker has access to over 300 of them, explaining in great detail why he'd be crazy to quit.

Control: Unlike time, money, etc.: something it's **fun** to be out of — at least until the Sun comes up.

Controlled Smoker: (see: **Unicorn; Tooth Fairy; Santa Claus**)

Cookie Cutter: Hand-held device used to stamp out the same boring shape, over and over again; found mainly in the homes of non-smokers (American Tobacco Institute Study; 1983).

"Cool:" A mellowness of lifestyle, attainable, like so many other things, by a lifetime of hard work or by simply mimicking someone allergic to same.

"Coop:" Nickname for film star Gary Cooper, who, among many other achievements, smoked himself to death.

Cop: Slang for "policeman:" someone with the power to make you do what you don't necessarily want to do, theoretically for the good of society; receives his power from the same pool that gives a smoker his sophistication (*which see*).

Cough: Violent attempt to expel material either blocking airways or tickling them; what smokers do a lot of, because of high humidity, low humidity, moderate humidity, nuclear fallout, but never because of their smoking habit.

Coughathon: A tender moment between a smoker and his toilet at the start and/or end of the day.

Coughing Jag: Extended bouts of coughing. To a non-smoker: cause for great alarm; to a smoker: his birthright (*which see*).

Courage: The bedrock of every smoker's personality, enabling him to face down death a hundred times a day without blinking — except, of course, if a tiny bit of smoke gets in his eye.

Covering a Base: In baseball: being in position to help your team achieve its objectives; in life: something you let someone else do, since doing it can result in "bad" things as well as "good" and who needs **that** hassle?!

Craving: Intense **physical** desire for something, created by your **psyche** (Subconscious Mind), and, therefore, impossible to "satisfy" **physically**; only possibility is to get your **psyche** to stop craving it, which you do by not giving in to its **physical** demands. Good luck.

Creative Juices: To a smoker: any nicotine-colored fluid;
To a non-smoker: orange, grapefruit...

Crocheting (pronounced: "crow-shay-ing"): Harmless pastime where you tie lots of knots in string, to create blouses, table cloths, dresser runners, etc.; what a lot of smokers would be a heck of a lot better off doing with their time.

Crybabies: Infantile people, forever complaining about how your smoking habit is ruining your health, ruining **their** health, stinking up the joint, burning holes in all the furniture — and otherwise doing everything in their power to make total nuisances of themselves.

Cub Scouts: Where boys 8-11 years old mark time until they can become full-fledged Boy Scouts, at which point most of them discover girls and are never heard from again.

Cyanide: Deadly poison — one of the few **not** found in cigarette smoke (unless the American Tobacco Institute has **really** been holding out on us!)

Cystic Fibrosis: Unavoidable hereditary disease characterized by, among other things, excess accumulation of mucus in the lungs.

Davis, Bette (pronounced "Betty"): Multiple Academy Award-winning actress, now dead, who often spent as much as 5 to 10 minutes of a two-hour movie **without** a cigarette in her mouth or hand.

Dead End: "Going nowhere of note;" typical of most people's jobs, habits, lives; reason for booming popularity of "worlds beyond!"

Dead-end Street: Where all addicts have their mail forwarded.

Death Sentence: Something that serial killers, spies and smokers spend their lives trying to get.

Decades: Ten-year periods. For our purposes: how long it usually takes smoking-related diseases to manifest themselves; also: how long you'll be dead because of them.

Deep Breathing: Main tool used by smokers who want to quit the habit; main thing avoided by smokers who don't.

Defining Yourself: Listing, in fairly complete fashion, who you are, how you like to "see" yourself, how you'd like the world to "see" you; best way known, to go from "smoker" to "non-smoker" or to stay right where you are.

Delicious: Word often used to describe: a) the way cigarettes taste; b) the way cigarette company **profits** "taste" to their shareholders.

Design Awards: What cigarette packagers and cigarette advertising agencies win lots of every year.

Dinner: Meal that a goodly number of dead people would probably like to have at least one more of.

Dinosaurs: Reptiles that dominated the animal world for over a hundred million years before becoming extinct about 65 million years ago — presumably through an excess of smoke in the air, the result of an Earth-asteroid collision.

Diorama: Depiction of a scene from real life, either full-size (museums) or in miniature (smoker's desk) (see also: **Vesuvius**).

"Distance:" Here: the amount of time between a smoker and his last cigarette; most powerful tool a smoker possesses for turning himself into a non-smoker.

Divorce Attorneys: Ex-squash players, now using a larger ball.

Doctor's Degree: What you need to possess before you can write prescriptions for drugs which, for the most part, help you; what you **don't** need to possess, to buy drugs which, for the most part, kill you (cigarettes; booze).

Donation: What you give to those less fortunate than yourself (see also: **Heart; Lungs; World Tobacco Cartel**).

Dorian Gray: Title character in Oscar Wilde novel — *The Portrait of Dorian Gray* — in which a painting of Mr. Gray, stowed carefully out of sight, keeps getting older and older, while its owner ages not a second, no matter how badly he treats himself and others — similar to the miracle each smoker hopes is taking place between him and the family photo album.

Downtown Park: Alternate residence-of-choice for homeless people (see also: **Freeway Overpass; Reagan, Ronald**).

Drag: Slang term for inhaling a quart of smoke from a burning cigarette; also: what lung cancer can very quickly become.

Draw: Money that salesman can "pull" against commissions earned; much easier to do when you're alive.

Dream World: Worry-free, disease-free, deliriously-happy universe created by the World Tobacco Cartel, that child smokers can't wait to live in.

Dre-e-e-eamy: What smokers think everybody else thinks they are.

Drug: Chemical that causes an organic change in the body. Normal usage: helping to cure disease; abnormal usage: round-trip ticket to Paradise, till the cable breaks.

Dull: Showing an uninteresting face to the world; of no concern to smokers, whose mind-numbing habit somehow keeps them sharp as a tack.

Dying by the Hour: Watching your life become **worse** off, as time goes by, due to constantly "living for the moment" (*which see*).

Earth: Incredibly-big, incredibly-important planet, while you're on it.

"Easier:" Not to be sneezed at, when "easy" is out to lunch.

East Jesus, Missouri: Mythical place that every grandmother in America goes to, to rock herself to sleep.

Eight Years Old: Age at which child first becomes of aware of cigarette advertising, if his parents didn't smoke (otherwise, see: **Six Hours Old**).

"Eighty-sixing:" Getting rid of.

Emphysema (pronounced: "Em-fah-zee-ma)**:** Disease where lung tissue finally stops wondering what it would have been like to be born as rawhide.

Employerus americansus **:** Species able to select the people he wants to work for him, since it's **his** company and it's **his** money that's paying everyone's salary, so who **better** to make the selections; now extinct.

Engineer (verb)**:** To manage a project and steer it in a definite direction.

Equal Time: What politicians demand from the media, so their opponents' lies don't wind up courting the electorate without a chaperon.

Eternity: Cosmologically: like, millions and millions of years.
To a smoker: the amount of time between cigarettes.

Everest: Fairly-tall mountain in Asia that's a lot easier to conquer if you **try** to.

Experimentation: What smokers can't wait to perform on their bodies every day, with hopes that the Nobel Prize committee won't lose their phone number.

Extinct Species List: Something growing at a rate the civilized world used to.

Famous Amos: Name of a tasty and popular chocolate chip cookie — among certain 300-pounders: **very** popular.

Faults: What everyone has and no one wants — especially the guy signing your paycheck.

Feathers: Delicate structures, found only on birds, which, when ruffled, make flying very difficult.

Female Independence: Feeling of having a "place in the Sun," which women can get by a lot of hard work or by staying in bed and lighting up a Virginia Slim.

Financial House: All you have of monetary value: savings, life insurance, medical insurance, stocks and bonds, etc., that you will be leaving for your family when you die.

Five Cents: What it costs to buy half a cigarette or produce a whole pack of them; also: about what your life will be worth if you don't stop smoking them.

Flies: Tiny little things that "drop" real easily if you use just the right poison (see also: **Lungs**).

Fluke: A chance occurrence that just happened spontaneously and could just as easily **not** have happened; often thought of as the way youngsters acquire their smoking habit. Other flukes of note, as catalogued by the American Tobacco Institute: Space Shuttle; Beethoven's Fifth Symphony; Western Civilization.

Food Absorption: What your body specializes in doing, from an unpoisoned small intestine — to the never-ending dismay of hot fudge sundae freaks.

Food Trough: Where abusive eaters spend a lot of **meal** time and the average smoker spends a lot of **post**-meal time.

Foot: Area toward the bottom of their body that people have a tendency to shoot themselves in, due to the ease of firing the gun but the difficulty of getting it out of the holster.

Forwarding Address: Where mail gets sent to, whether or not there's anyone home to read it.

Free: What we'd love everything to be but what nothing ever is (see also: **Black and White**).

Freeway Overpass: Residence-of-choice for homeless people (see also: **Downtown Park; Reagan, Ronald**).

Frenching (Smoke): Involved process of first taking smoke into your mouth and then leaking it back out to your nose, which you then use to inhale it into your lungs. Main value: making sure Eye-ear-nose-and-throat men get a new Cadillac **every** year, rather than every **other** year.

Frenchmen (Fifty million): Large group of Europeans who have had an undue influence over what the rest of the world does, due to their creation of the "safety-in-numbers" concept (*which see*).

Friendship: Provided by warm, glowing people or warm, glowing cigarettes.

Fun: A sense of joy; what losers go for in the short run, winners over the long haul.

Funding: What most institutions are so afraid of losing, they'll go to any lengths to keep it — sometimes, even, what they were funded to do to begin with.

Game: A word that brings to mind an innocent, sometimes challenging activity we all have fond memories of playing (see also: **Hopscotch; Dominoes; Russian Roulette; State Lottery**).

Garden Slug: Highest possible conversational level attainable by non-smokers (see also: **Bogey**).

Gas Lines: Long strings of cars waiting for gasoline in 1973-4 and 1979 America, due, we were told, to Arabs refusing to ship us oil (see also: **Autofocus Cameras**).

Gasoline: Chemical produced by big oil companies (*which see*).

Geeks: Strange inhabitants of the non-smoking world; exhibit tendency to outlive **non**-geeks by an average of 10 to 20 years (see also: **Wimps**).

Genes: The little things inside your cells that determine what you'll be long before you have a chance to. Since you get them from your parents, whatever bad things they had to put up with you probably will, too. Sorry.

Genetic: Referring to your genes (*which see*).

Genius: Person able to see connections between things that other people can't; apparently, America's no-deposit, no-return gift to the world.

Genius of the Year Award: Prestigious prize, most often self-awarded.

Getting Run Over (by a Bus): Super argument smokers use, to justify continuing their habit: "After all, why should I quit smoking when I'll probably be getting run over by a bus anyway, sometime in the next 10, 20 minutes, so what have I saved? Dead is dead, isn't it?"

Glop: What **everybody** coughs up every day or every year, so why blame smoking?

Glop Accumulation: What your lungs specialize in, if you'll just help them.

Goal: A target you're shooting for: the more defined it is, the easier it is to hit.

Golf: Croquet in Hell.

"Good ol'": Chummy prefix, commonly applied to mean, bigoted, backward individuals or institutions.

"Good Sex:" Term difficult to define; more research needed.

Gorbachev, Mikhail Sergeyevich: Soviet leader ousted in the "Long-Weekend Coup" of 1991; returned to (diminished) power three days later.

Gordian Knot: A knot so difficult to untie that no one can do it; see also: Spanish word for "fat."

Government Subsidies: Money handed out by the government when you don't make as much as you wanted to; schools currently taking notes from tobacco growers and arms manufacturers on how to get some.

Grade School: Where most children don't smoke and still don't want to.

Grief: What quitting smoking leads to for a few days; also: what **not** quitting smoking leads to in a few years.

Gross National Product: The total monetary value of the goods and services a nation produces.

Grown-ups: People who always know what they're doing, until you become one; also: what all young smokers want to be — and **keep** wanting to be till the day they die.

Gun: What the cigarette companies don't have to hold to your head to get you using their products; what you'll be thinking of holding to **their** head when the biopsy results come back .

Gutter: Final resting place, at the edge of street or roof, for all the trash that natural forces can pull down into it (see also: **Smoking; Doing Drugs; Boozing; Gambling; Child Abuse;..............**)

Guts: Reputed residence of intestinal fortitude (*which see*).

Gypsies: Historically: Nomadic people whose lack of geographic permanence made them "immune" to the laws and social niceties of whatever community they happened to be passing through that week.

Habit: What you do unconsciously, day after day. Since they are **un**conscious, can only be broken and replaced by **conscious effort**. Once the old habit is "broken," the new habit becomes as unconscious and hard to break as the old one.

Half a Brain: Sole requirement for giving up smoking; also: what a lot of people would give their eye teeth to have if they only knew it.

Half-century: Approximate length of time it takes for smoking-related diseases to find you and kill you— unless you push it.

Hankies: Short for "handkerchiefs:" pieces of cloth used to keep tears from staining expensive caskets.

Hard Drugs: Rarely-advertised drugs you need a prescription or pusher to get and that sometimes kill you (see also: **Soft Drugs**).

Havoc: What nicotine and tar specialize in playing with your innards.

Healing Power (of the Brain): Miraculous ability of the brain to let bygones **really** be bygones, unlike everyone else you've ever met.

Health, Financial: Primary concern of big tobacco companies, big oil companies, etc. (*which see*).

Health Insurance: The way smokers get non-smokers to pay for smoking-related diseases.

Heart: Muscular pump that keeps you alive — itself kept alive by itsy-bitsy, teeny-weeny arteries that feed it food and oxygen between cigarettes.

Heart Attack: Sudden closure of the arteries that feed your heart muscle life-giving oxygen, often resulting in instant death; also: something which smoking could never be the cause of (American Tobacco Institute Study, soon to be published).

Helm: Where an organization's course is "steered;" smoker's is very crowded, but with no one he knows well enough to ask over for dinner.

Helter-Skelter (of Daily Life): High-pressure situations that smokers use, to justify continuing their habit; what non-smokers can't wait to become part of every day.

Heroin: Highly-addictive drug that you have to take over and over again in the beginning, till you finally stop getting sick from it and can start getting hooked by it (see also: **Cigarettes; Booze; etc.**)

High: Feeling that drugs can give you; also: cost of treating diseases drugs can give you; also: cost of funerals from diseases drugs can give you.

Himmler, Heinrich (1900-1945): Rodent-faced head of the Gestapo in Nazi Germany; responsible for implementation of the "Final Solution" to the "Jewish Problem" — and a lot of other problems you tend to run into when you've had the misfortune of not being born on your very own planet. Greatest crime: only able to die once, regardless the number he killed.

Hitting below the Belt: An action that will either get you disqualified in a boxing match or win you the bout, depending on who sees you and who doesn't.

Hooked (on cigarettes): What someone assured you you absolutely couldn't get — right up to the moment you did (see also: **Cocaine; Heroin; Booze; Gambling; Sweets;.............**)

Hope, Bob: Nickname: "Ski Nose." Very popular, highly-patriotic comedian/entertainer, currently trying to outlive God and better-than-even-money to do so.

Horror: Cold feeling of dread, caused by looking at a smoker's lungs or R. J. Reynolds's bank account.

Horseshoe: Good luck symbol enthusiastically endorsed by the National Rabbit Association.

Hot Fudge Sundae: God's gift to abusive eaters who have earned a "treat," by, for example, opening a door, turning on a light all by themselves, watching leaves fall.......

Human Chimney: My former nickname; source of inestimable pride, till I buried my four pack-a-day father.

Human Nature: What you can count on your neighbor doing; the brand of Silly Putty future advertising executives are given to play with, on their 5th birthday.

Hurdle: Barrier that has to first be overcome before you can continue on your way toward a goal; in giving up cigarettes: lifetime of familiarity; chemical addiction; number of associates who continue smoking; advertising that makes smoking seem chic and acceptable; etc. (see also: **Everest**).

Hussein, Saddam: Kindly-looking current leader of Iraq who apparently tried to cancel out war debt with Kuwait by cancelling out Kuwait. Severely punished for his actions by having his people blown back to the Stone Age by American and allied troops.

IBM Mainframe: Powerful computing device, absolutely indispensable in keeping track of tobacco company profits, of no Earthly use to your average stop-smoking program.

Identity: Everything about you that **is** you; the way you "see" yourself; the way you'd like others to "see" you; easy to form, but difficult to change — just ask somebody.

"I'll Play These:" Poker term for indicating that you'll just play the cards you were dealt, with no need to find out what **else** the deck might have to offer.

Illusion: What magicians count on, to get you to buy their program (see also: **Big Tobacco Companies**).

Impression: Best Case: What you make on others.
                          If "Best Case" not working: What you make on yourself.

Impulse: Something that gets you going from "A" to "B."

Informed Decision: A better way of determining your life's course.

Inhale: To take into your lungs; also: young smoker's Rubicon (*which see*).

Insult: What you do to your body when you fill it with noxious foreign substances; also: what tobacco company advertising does to the intelligence of ex-smokers.

Intestinal Fortitude: Mystical concept once thought to be the birthright of every human being; now known to have just been "gas."

Iron Lung: Whole-body device created in the 1920's to breathe for people who had lost the ability to do so on their own — especially polio victims; now accomplished by other means (ventilators; respirators).

Jelly Donut *Flambé* : Nonsensical food creation that a legion of smokers will now try to reproduce, just to inhale the fumes.

Jerk: Someone born to do non-hip things — among which: to outlive hip smokers, hip drug addicts, hip alcoholics, etc.

Jews: Small group of people that a good portion of the world would apparently like to see grow even smaller, due to group members' bizarre beliefs and rituals (not drinking themselves to death; making enough money to stay off welfare; educating their children to within an inch of their lives; winning a disproportionate number of Nobel Prizes; trying — often overzealously and always unpolitically — to carve out a piece of world soil where they might **not** get thrown into a gas chamber; etc.)

Job One: The most important thing to do, of all the things you could be doing.

Jogging: What smokers watch non-smokers do, from the safety of their front porch (see also: **Biking; Thinwalking; Rollerblading; etc.**).

Johnnie Walker Red: Less expensive Scotch Whiskey than Johnnie Walker Black (colors refer to labels) or Chivas Regal (*which see*).

Joy: Feeling of elation you get when you do hard things right or hard drugs at night.

Junkie: Originally: Heroin addict; now: almost any old addict will do.

Kinship: A warm feeling of fellowship with those around you; automatic among smokers; totally unknown between non-smokers.

Knees: Body structures that tend to lose their weight-bearing capacity in the presence of smoking movie stars — even the ones living in Central Park.

Knife: What robbers and Marlboros are fond of sticking between your ribs.

Knowledge: Can be the same as power, if you know you've got it; also: the first brick on the road to change.

Kohlberg, Kravis & Roberts: Wall Street firm that specializes in helping rich people buy out other rich people, with the resulting benefit to society rarely requiring a Richter Scale to measure it.

Kuwait: Tiny, oil-rich country at the tip of Iraq that the latter tried to bring back into the fold in the Autumn of 1990, much to the consternation of Kuwaiti leadership and about three billion tons of American and allied bombs.

LSD: Lysergic acid diethylamide. Hallucinogenic drug favored by people in the 1960's who wanted to find out how much of the Universe they could visit without the bother of going to Cape Canaveral.

Last Gasp: Type of attempt your mind and body make, to get you to hold on to a habit; also: sound frequently heard in lung cancer and emphysema wards.

Laws of Nature: Unbreakable edicts that you can use to your advantage or watch your neighbor use to **his**.

Lawsuit: Civilization by other means.

Leary, Timothy: Charismatic Harvard psychologist of the 1960's, who recommended the use of LSD (*which see*) to "tune in, turn on, drop out" — which many Americans did, until the military and industry saw their "bottom **line** 'dropping out'" and had the drug placed on the "Boy-is-**this**-a-bad-one" list.

Ledge: Where **real** suicides spend very little of their time; where smokers stand perched every minute of their lives.

Lemmings: Furry little Norwegian animals who commit mass suicide every so often by diving into the ocean without their Red Cross Certificates (see also: **Safety-in-Numbers Concept**).

Leveraged Buyout: Using the value of what you're **buying** as collateral for the loan to buy it. Theoretically, then, average Skid Row denizen could buy the Taj Mahal — and one day will, if Kohlberg, Kravis & Roberts have anything to say about it.

"Librium:" Trade name for "diazepoxide:" a compound originally devised as a muscle relaxer, but now, along with its "son," Valium, the most successful **tranquilizers** of all time.

Lid: Something that fits best on Mason jars and infantile impulses.

Life: What a smoker pours his habit into.

Life-expectancy "Numbers" (on Fat People): One of the 28 major reasons smokers use, to justify never giving up their habit.

Lightheadedness: Disturbing though temporary feeling that ex-smokers get, when lung passages that haven't seen the light of day for hundreds of pack-years (*which see*), suddenly burst open again (or "for the first time," if your parents smoked).

Little Children: Small people who need to give in to every impulse that cries out for attention; who suck constantly on pacifiers; and whose bed linens need constant changing, because of the smell (see also: [guess]).

Living for the Moment: The most fun way to live (see also: **Dying by the Hour**).

Livelihood: What you make, unless you can con someone else into making it **for** you.

Long Run, the: Constantly on the mind of adults; of absolutely no concern to children.

Long-term Destruction: The trade-off all out-of-control people "can't wait" to make.

Long-term Satisfaction: The result of exerting some control over childish impulses.

Loser: Someone getting the least out of life or the most, depending on who you're talking to at the time.

Losing Streak: What all sports teams experience some of the time; what all smokers experience all of the time; what the families of all smokers experience once.

***Lost Weekend*:** 1940's movie starring Ray Milland in an Academy Award-winning performance as an alcoholic going through the horrors of withdrawing from his addiction.

Lottery, State: A "fun" thing — a "game" that welfare mothers try to trade their food stamps and WIC coupons to "play," but one which, statistically speaking, no one ever wins; also: a much grander way to finance State education than by hitting up your average millionaire for about a thousandth of his net worth.

Love-in: Term whose main value is to date the author; gathering where lots of people would express their love for one another, or for a society they all dreamed of creating; soon discovered to be impractical for doing either.

Loves of your Life: Full size: spouse, children, friends, relatives, etc.   Small size: Lucky's, Marlboro's, Parliament's, Benson & Hedges, etc.

Luck of the Draw: Normally: something impossible to influence; main reason, according to them, that smokers get lung cancer, alcoholics get cirrhosis of the liver, heroin addicts keep rewriting the How-long-can-you-hold-your-breath record book, etc.

Lucky's: Abbreviation for Lucky Strike — cigarette produced by the American Tobacco Company. Favorite advertising line: "It's toasted;" some question as to whether they're referring to **their** tobacco or **your** lung. Other classic advertising phrase: "L. S./M. F. T." Not sure what the "T" refers to, but have certain ideas about the "M. F."

Lunacy: Form of insanity, originally thought to be influenced by the moon, but humans now known to need no help at all.

Lunatics: People first in line when the DMV opens.

Lung Cancer: "The only cancer you can get from smoking" (source: common knowledge; thus, no need to see: **Mouth Cancer; Tongue Cancer; Throat Cancer; Esophageal Cancer; Stomach Cancer;............**).; also: delightful disease that when it first shows up on X-ray is already too late to cure.

Lung Cells, Ciliated: Little cells in your lungs with "hairs" on their head that "sweep" the crud up from the depths of your lungs to a place where you can cough it out, if you'll just let them; the reason coughing **increases** when you quit smoking.

Lung Passages: Teeny openings in your lungs that'll be happy to clean themselves out, anytime you're ready.

Macho: Spanish word denoting "male strength;" possibly a contraction of the word *muchacho* : "boy." If so, then apparently it takes the **loss** of something to turn a boy into a man.

Magic: Where things that "can't happen" suddenly seem to; about the only thing that cancer victims, emphysemics, etc., can rely on to return them to full health.

***Magnificent Seven, the*:** Western movie starring Yul Brynner; also, to their investors: the big oil companies and the big tobacco companies.

***Man with a Golden Arm* :** 1950's movie starring Academy Award-winner Frank Sinatra as a poker dealer with a heroin habit.

Manager: Someone who gets the most or the least out of those he's managing, depending on what he can get out of himself.

Marathon: A 26.2-mile race, which every smoker in the world will tell you how dangerous it is to run.

Marlboro Cigarettes: Product of the Philip Morris Company. Best-selling cigarette in the world. Gave that world a new version of the "flip-top box" — a little smaller than the one that undertakers were used to.

Marlboro Man: Hard-roping, hard-living, tattoo-handed hero, who somehow manages to puff away on cigarettes while doing things that would tax the lungs of marathon runners. Original Marlboro Man lived well into his 80's before passing away, thus giving new lease on life to whole generation of Marlboro smokers, who think you're talking about a whale's tail when you mention the word "fluke."

Mars: Fourth planet out from the Sun, which the U. S. and Russians are about to spend 40 zillion dollars going to, for reasons known only to Ray Bradbury and 23 rockhounds in Missoula, Montana.

Marsh Grass: Apparently, the source of cheap pipe tobacco.

Meal, a: "Just food," to a non-addict;

"Food-plus-a-cigarette," to a smoker;

"Food-plus-a-beer," to an alcoholic;

"Food-plus-dessert," to an abusive eater;

"The Racing Form-and-a-cup-of-coffee," to a horse-player.

Medals: Things which people pin on their chests when no one else wants to.

Medical Profession: Group of intelligent guys and gals who, ideally, spend a good deal of time praying to God to heal the bodies that He, not they, created.

Metastatic: Spreading like wildfire; refers almost always to "cancer."

Michaelangelo Buonarotti: Italian sculptor whose life was popularized, ironically enough, by Irving **Stone**.

Microscope: A handy tool to have, when you want to see how badly life is treating you, as compared to your average Ethiopian.

Mid-South: Area of the United States containing Virginia, North Carolina, Kentucky, Tennessee.

Milk: Life-sustaining fluid that has a disturbing tendency to attract flies; also: something that tastes terrible with cigarettes (see, for contrast: **Coffee; Beer; Wine; Scotch...**)

Million-Dollar Slots: Something which I'm sure everybody can beat, if they just play long enough (see also: **Lottery; Russian Roulette; Smoking**).

Minefield: In war: a stretch of land or water where explosives are laid, to discourage an enemy force from advancing to a forward position. In everyday life: what a smoker's lungs, heart, stomach, etc., have to pray their way through, every time he lights up.

Mirror: Piece of silvered glass reflecting your soul, if you know where to look.

Mite: A small quantity; derived from animal of the same name.

Moral: What every good story should have, so we can learn something from it; otherwise, it's wallpaper.

Movie: Best way of seeing things that have already happened; useful mental device for smokers trying to see themselves as non-smokers.

Murphy's Law (Original): "If anything can go wrong, it will."

Murphy's Law of Non-Smokers: "No matter where a non-smoker sits, he will always be directly in the path of any and all smoke."

Murphy's Law of Quitting Smoking: "Everything that could possibly go wrong in your life will wait until you've decided to quit smoking before doing so."

Naive (pronounced: "nah-yeev"): Not knowing as much as you think you know, and a lot less than everyone you **know** knows.

National Debt: A number so high no one can count to it.

"Natural:" What smoking definitely isn't, no matter how much it **feels** like it is, after 20 years of doing it.

Necktie Party: A public hanging — and we ain't talking "macramé!"

New Lease on Life: What a new manager can give you, especially if it's **you**.

Nickel: Denomination of American currency that used to actually buy something (see also: **Five Cents**).

Nicotine: Schizophrenic drug that can't decide if it's better at squeezing off life-giving arteries or killing off millions of nerve cells. One billion smokers now doing field research to decide the issue once and for all.

Night of the Living Dead: Popular horror movie of the 1950's, whose title is fairly self-explanatory.

Nightmare: A bad dream you "can't wait" to wake up from, but sometimes have to.

Ninety-Three Per Cent: Number of doctors **hired by the American Tobacco Institute** to prove that smoking is "harmless," who finally said: "It's nothing of the kind! It'll kill you!"; those 93% currently under investigation by the remaining 7% to see if they are, in fact, doctors of medicine or, as is the current suspicion, doctors of musicology or perhaps dental hygiene.

Nirvana: Hindu Heaven, where nicotine takes smokers, under a Frequent Flyer plan.

Nixon, Richard: Thirty-seventh President of the United States. An obvious crook and sleazebag his entire political career, he was finally brought to justice (well, real close) because of his involvement in the 1972 break-in of Democratic National Headquarters at the Watergate Hotel near Washington, D. C.

Non-smoker: Someone not getting anywhere **near** the enjoyment he **could** be getting out of life, if he'd just pay a bit more attention to the glorious cigarette ads; also: what your Subconscious Mind (*which see*) automatically makes you, if you stay off cigarettes for a long, long time (7 days; maybe 14, tops).

Non-smoking Friends: Difficult for a smoker to find, even though there are about 4 billion to choose from.

Non-smoking Life: Source of unending terror to a smoker, unending joy to a "used-to-be" smoker.

Non-smoking Restaurants: Birthplace of the Smokers Rights movement; also: places where the **food** is the only potentially-lethal item left on the menu.

Non-smoking Wimps: Junior high school crowd you instantly soared above, with your first cigarette.

Nonchalance: A laid-back attitude exhibited by million-dollar movie stars and pre-teens puffing away on their first cigarette.

North Carolina: State where cigarettes are real cheap (see also: **Life**).

Noxious Chemicals: Fumes inhaled by folks in Gary, Indiana, and a smoker's bathroom.

No. 10 Brake Line: Material most often used to stop cars and allow smoking **inside** a shower.

Oddball: Strange person who does strange things to himself, like not destroying his body 24 hours a day.

Offensive: Verb: Attack
　　　　　Adjective: Everything about smoking to a non-smoker.

Old Reliable: Something you can always count on (see also: **Family Dog; Sun Coming Up; Nicotine**).

Older People: Folks whose time would be better spent **not** listing all the mistakes they've made in their lives, for all the good it will be doing the next generation.

Olympics: The Olympic Games: a gathering of nations, every four years, to engage in athletic competitions; "Siberia," to a cigarette salesman.

"Only Here Once:" Perfect reason for doing "any damn thing you please!" Also: perfect reason for **not** doing it.

"Oral:" A psychological condition where you need near-constant stimulation in the area of your mouth; fourteen smokers worldwide have now been confirmed as suffering from this condition.

Origami: Ancient Japanese art of paper-folding.
                  Beginners Level: Swans and stuff
                  Intermediate Level: Marlboro box
                  Advanced Level: Stealth Bomber

Oxygen: Active ingredient in air (*which see*), unless you're a plant or planted.

Oz: Fantasy world created by Frank Baum to give tobacco companies the model they needed for the world their products can take you to.

Pacifier: What you use, to stay calm; often made of the same indestructible rubber or plastic as a smoker's lungs.

Pack-year: Number of packs of cigarettes you smoke each day multiplied by the number of years you've smoked them. Example: 2 packs per day for 20 years = 40 pack-years. "Twenty pack-years" generally considered to be the minimum amount of time necessary to begin generating smoking-related disease — except, of course, when it's not (family history of cancer, emphysema, stroke, etc.)

Pain: What your undertaker's banker starts to get, when he finds out you've quit smoking.

Palate: The roof of your mouth, where food races smoke to see which can get to a cigarette fiend's throat first.

Panache: A confident way of interacting with people and relating to life; also: something often mistakenly asked for at Spanish wine-tastings.

***Panic in Needle Park*:** 1960's movie starring Al Pacino as a heroin addict facing "dry" times rather than "high" times in "Needle Park."

Parents: The people who gave you everything you've got. Be sure you remember to thank them between smokes, or between drinks, or between bets, or between cookies, or between........

Passenger Pigeons: Bird that used to number in the billions; now extinct.

Passion: Intense feelings exhibited toward a person, place or thing; often felt as strongly by ex-smokers toward their **new** "habit" as by smokers toward their existing one.

Pawning Off: An easy way to get rid of your problems; first step in making sure you stay right where you are.

Pension Funds: What a lot of corporate and government employees close their eyes and contribute to every year, in hopes they won't still have to be shoveling milk in their late 80's (see also: **Lottery**).

Penthouses: Places real high up in apartment buildings or office buildings, where birds of prey often nest, since it gives them the best view they could possibly have of their next victims.

Phone Call: Responsible for more cigarettes being lit each day than all the coughs in Carolina (see also: **Starting your Car; Brushing your Teeth; Finishing a Meal; etc.**)

"Pink-Slipped:" Historically: the way employees find out they've been fired: by the inclusion of such a message on a pink slip of paper in their pay envelope.

Pit: Half of an Edgar Allen Poe title — *The Pit and the Pendulum* — about a man in a dungeon, strapped to a table, with a razor-sharp pendulum swinging back and forth over him, getting closer and closer to his chest with each swing (see also: **Smoking Cigarettes**).

Plunge: Sometimes, the only way to get into the water.

Poison: A good way to keep from slowing down in old age.

Polio: Viral disease that kills cells in the central nervous system (brain and spinal cord); now pretty well eliminated, due to worldwide vaccination (see also: **Iron Lung**).

Politician: Human being intensely desirous of serving the people he used to live among, for what amounts, relatively speaking, to no financial gain whatsoever; unique ability to speak out of both sides of his mouth makes him greatly in demand for circus sideshows when 50-year term in Congress has run its course.

Pope, the: "Good Catholic" who lives in Vatican City and who a lot of people would apparently like to take a shot at and one actually did!

Power: What drugs and knowledge can give you.

Prayer: Making a request of God to please not treat you nearly so badly as you're treating yourself; also: the main thing joining you to God, or, in the case of a smoker, the main thing keeping you from joining Him too **soon**.

Pride: Good feelings about yourself that you get from doing things well.

Pride of the Yankees: 1942 film starring Gary Cooper and Teresa Wright (later, an apparently unhappy **Mrs.** Cooper) about the life of New York Yankee first baseman Lou Gehrig, who played in a record 2,130 consecutive games before being diagnosed as having amyotrophic lateral sclerosis — known, since that time, as "Lou Gehrig's Disease" — and succumbing from it two years after playing his last game.

Princess Bride, the: Delightful movie of the mid-1980's, written by William Goldman, in which one of the characters — "Miracle Max," played by Billy Crystal — has a lot easier time performing his "miracles" on people who are just "**mostly** dead," rather than those who've traveled to the end of the line.

"Pros" (as in "Pros and Cons"): Reasons for doing something (see also: **"Cons"**); also: what people feel like when they quit smoking.

150   *Dying for a Smoke*

Prude: Someone with unreasonable objections to joining the with-it world (see also: **Smoking; Drinking; Gambling;..........**).

Psychological Addiction: The **real** reason tobacco company executives have such lovely *dachas* in the Carolina countryside.

Puberty: Something that usually begins about the age of 12 and lasts for a few years in non-abusers or a few decades in alcoholics, obesics, smokers, gamblers, junkies................

Public Opinion: What you have to drink every last drop of, before distilling your own.

Public School: Where lots and lots of people go every year for an education and where a couple, three, actually get one.

Quality Jobs: Enjoyable, challenging ways to spend your money-earning years; almost the exclusive province of non-smokers (see also: **Quality Spouses; Quality Schools; etc.**).

Rabbit's Foot: Traditional good-luck symbol, though some question among rabbit population as to propriety of the designation; along with prayer: main medical means smokers use, to keep themselves completely free of disease (see also: **Horseshoe**).

Railing: Synonym for ranting and raving; source of great amusement to tobacco company executives when done by irate customers.

Reagan, Ronald: Fortieth President of the United States. Famous for statement: "The homeless people are homeless because they **want** to be homeless!"

Reasoner, Harry (d. 1991): One of the original, and apparently one of the "kindest" correspondents on CBS News' highly-popular *60 Minutes* newsmagazine, who donated his life to a two pack-a-day habit.

Red Numbers: Things that go up on a golf scoreboard, to indicate that you are below par — which is good — in contrast to **feeling** below par, which is bad. Go figure.

Reform School: Prison-like educational institution, formerly reserved for criminal types, now found on any inner-city street corner.

Relaxing: Unwinding from a hectic day of autofocus cameras, remote control TV's, automatic door openers, computerized bookkeeping, cruise-controlled cars, self-cleaning ovens, frost-free refrigerators, etc. Often requires a strong drug, to get maximum benefit from.

Remote Controls: God's gift to weight-loss clinics.

Renoir, Pierre Auguste (1841-1919)**:** French Impressionist; used to trade paintings for free rent; could now rent the Taj Mahal for what paintings fetch.

Rent Money: An amount of currency so small, compared to the fortunes it can bring, that average gambler has "no problem" betting it away every month.

Research Dollars: What the American Tobacco Institute spends millions of every year, trying to prove how harmless an activity smoking is (for how much money that will **really** take, see: "There ain't that much money in the World, Jack!").

Retard (pronounced: "**re**-tard")**:** What tobacco company executives pray everyone suddenly turns into, when coming across one of their ads.

Reunion: Joyous time, when you get back together with loved ones; happens every 10 years for high school classmates, every 10 minutes for substance abusers.

Reynolds, R. J.: Company in North Carolina whose cutesy-pie camel (*which see*) lulls millions to sleep each night — including, rumor has it, a few adults.

Ritual: Something we do over and over again, until it becomes as comfortable and "natural" to do as breathing, so that giving it up would be the **same** as giving up breathing, so we don't.

Robber Barons: American royalty.

Rolled-up Plant: Synonym for "cigarette:" a mini-computer pre-programmed to help you determine the course your life will take.

Roping (steers): Skill apparently acquired automatically with first pack of Marlboros.

Rubicon: River in Northern Italy that Caesar crossed in 49 B.C., to start civil war with Pompey, after which there was "no turning back."

Russian Roulette: Game in which revolver has only one bullet in the six chambers. Cylinder is spun, then handed to the next player, who puts gun to his head and pulls the trigger (see also: **Smoking**).

S. O. P.: "Standard Operating Procedure."

Safety-in-Numbers: Delightful thought, if it were true; guiding philosophy of most lemming populations (*which see*).

St. Peter: The guy manning the pearl-covered check-in desk at Heavenly Hacienda.

Salem: Name of a city in Massachusetts where people were burned as witches at the end of the 17th century; also: name of a cigarette that people burn for R. J. Reynolds riches in the late 20th century.

Saliva: Alternate residence-of-choice for nicotine and tar (see also: **Lungs**).

Sanskrit: Ancient Asian language that underlings are frequently accused of specializing in.

Satisfaction: Good feeling that comes from living the way you should.

Saturated: What your bloodstream is with nicotine, after your first cigarette of the day; also: what your average national magazine is, with ads for same.

Scare Tactics: Favored device of anti-smoking activists trying to get smoking friends and relatives to quit; cause of more short-term deafness in smokers than the next five diseases combined.

School: Place where youngsters try to outimpress one another with everything going on in their lives — except, for some reason, how **educated** they're getting; also: places where administrators spend a good deal of time determining how many innovative programs they can keep out.

Schwarzenegger, Arnold: Big guy who should really stop smoking those cigars, but **you** tell him!

Scoring Position: Where you at least have to get to, to be most likely to score when the next good thing happens (in baseball: being on second base, so you can get home on a single).

Scurvy: Disease caused by deficiency of Vitamin C; cured by being in the same room with an orange. Rumored to be under investigation by the American Tobacco Institute as the "Number One Cause of Preventable Death in the Known Universe."

Searing Heat: Commonly used to cook steaks, chops and lungs.

Secretariat: One of the greatest racehorses that ever lived; winner of the 1973 Triple Crown: Kentucky Derby/Preakness/Belmont — the last by a 31-length margin over the **second**-place horse!

Sedation: Calm feeling that comes from **doing** something right or from taking the right **drug**.

Self-Respect: The feeling you get when you do what's right; only prerequisite: knowing what that is.

Selfish: The best reason for doing anything, no matter what anyone tells you.

Semi-Fast: Walking speed that a rocking chair can't hope to keep up with.

Seventh-Day Adventists: Christian group that finds it extremely difficult to stop trying to keep the human race from killing itself, with high-fat meats, low-fat cigarettes, etc.

Sherman: General William Tecumseh Sherman, American Civil War leader who decided to share his mid-War nervous breakdown with the good folks of Georgia.

Shill: Person paid by a company to promote its product(s); not to be confused with "swill:" a vile liquid, often very hard to swallow.

Shining Armor: What knights wore who rode out from King Arthur's castle on noble missions; what the world could use a little more of, if it weren't so damned expensive.

Shopping Malls: Latter-day Parthenons, but with fewer public restrooms.

Shortfall: What every little capitalist spends his sleeping hours dreaming of making up for; what every big capitalist spends his waking hours dreaming of ways to create.

Sideshow: In a circus: the place where lesser acts are forced to perform; to a smoker: what his non-smoking life is.

Silver Screen: Large piece of cloth, specially-treated to glamorize smoking to pre-pubescent Detroiters.

Silverware: Household utensils most often taken by uninvited guests; what smokers wish their habit **would** have taken, when the test results come back.

Sis-Boom-Bah: Favorite rallying cry of your average cheering section; most often heard from smokers rooting for other smokers to continue their habit, so they won't go down alone.

Six Hours Old: Age at which your lungs "saw" their first cigarette ad, if one or more of your parents smoked.

Skin: "Dead tissue" that's really only **mostly** dead and thus can be made even **deader**, if you try hard enough (see also: *The Princess Bride*).

Slacks: Article of clothing extremely difficult to get on over your head.

Slavery: Living under the complete control of someone or something other than yourself; in which case, some question as to the propriety of the word "living."

Smiling: Honest activity among people who've learned to exert some control over their lives; counterfeit activity among smokers, drinkers, abusive eaters, gamblers, drug addicts, etc.

Smoker: Heroic figure who would call you "crazy" if you went to the leading edge of a brushfire and gulped down gallons of the gray glop billowing forth from the conflagration.

Smoker's Cough: Nearly-continuous attempt by the body to rid itself of vile lung crud; formerly thought to be caused by smoking, now known to be the result of pollen allergies and the alignment of Jupiter's middle six moons (American Tobacco Institute Study, soon to be released).

Smoker's Lung: Safe deposit box for a smoker's most treasured memories.

Smokers' Rights Organizations: Lobbying groups with no apparent connection to any tobacco companies, formed to make sure smokers don't get "buried" by an increasingly-hostile non-smoking world (see also: **Boozers' Rights Organizations; Junkies' Rights Organizations; Serial-Killers' Rights Organizations;.................**).

Smoking: Activity that allows instantaneous transformation from: wimp to worldly; sop to sophisticate; baby to Bogie.

Smoking Opportunity: Similar to a "photo opportunity," but occasionally a tad deadlier.

Smoking Yarns: Exciting stories of smokers' exploits. Some classics: "Great Cigarettes I Have Known;" "The Freeway Dance of the Fallen Ember;" "Dying your Whole House Yellow with just a Flick of your Bic;" etc.

Snail Darter: Cute little fish that only lives in one small pool in Death Valley, California. As of this writing, the Valley is a "lock" to outlive the fish.

"Snowing:" Another word for "impressing:" refers to "burying" someone under an "avalanche" of your talents.

Social Convention: The thing that keeps non-addicts in a rut.

Soft Drugs: Heavily-advertised drugs that you don't need a prescription or pusher to get (any convenience store will do) and that will **always** kill you (see also: **Hard Drugs**).

Solar System: Our Sun and its nine planets and millions of comets and zillions of asteroids. Our planet is third from the Sun, Mars is fouth, Jupiter — East **and** West — is fifth, and the rest are so far away you don't know anyone there anyway.

Sophistication: What you achieve when all the "rough edges" have been rubbed off or smoked off.

Spic n' Span: Popular home cleaner.

Spoon, Needle, Rubber Hose, Matches: Paraphernalia used by junkie (*which see*), to fix heroin and then himself.

Springtime: Beautiful time of the year that smokers seem to be trying to give themselves as few of as possible.

Stalin, Josef (1879-1953)**:** Fatherly leader of the Soviet Union, who, when he was finished slaughtering the 23 million of his own people who refused to collectivize their farms, uttered the now-famous: "That'll learn 'em!", or whatever that works out to in Russian.

"Statement:" What smokers make with their habit, every minute they're alive; what non-smokers **never** make, but for a hell of a lot longer!

Status Quo: "OK: no one move and you won't get hurt!" (line from *Bonnie and Clyde [which see]*).

Step: What smokers are dead certain they haven't lost a single one of, so "why would I go out there and make a fool of myself like all those 'jogging' nincompoops?"

Stress: What "pressure" leads to; feeling of being "under the gun;" relieved by doing whatever it takes to pull out the clip ("finishing the assignment," for example), or by putting a piece of toilet paper over the end of the barrel ("taking a drug").

Stroke: Also known as "apoplexy:" gradual or rapid rupturing of a blood vessel in the brain, leading to paralysis or death. Usually caused by high blood pressure, which can be the result of many things — smoking among them.

Success: What everyone should have as his goal, without having to be talked into it.

Sue: Attempt to get monetary restitution for having been wronged by another; prime source of entertainment at the major tobacco companies.

Suicide: Killing yourself.

       Short form: cyanide; .357; testing anti-gravity devices from 40 stories up.

       Long form: Chesterfields.

Sunspots: Black spots seen on photos of the Sun, now known to be the primary cause of black spots seen on photos of the lung (American Tobacco Institute Study, soon to be released).

Survival: The only reason your Subconscious Mind is around.

Swindlers: Smooth-voiced gentlemen who can always round up a lot more money than you can.

Table Manners: Constant concern of smokers, in the children of non-smokers.

Tar: Sticky black stuff, used to coat roofs, roads and lungs.

Target: What you're shooting at; impossible to hit till you know where it's at.

Tattoo: Latter-day stigma that has been known to appear spontaneously on the hands of Marlboro disciples.

Taylor, Robert: Incredibly-handsome movie star. Real name: Spangler Arlington Brugh. One of the world's great on-screen lovers and off-screen smokers. Now dead — and trust us: it wasn't from too much **loving**!

Tearing Clothing: A sign of great grief; also: what a smoker should do after every carton, to see if **that** will get rid of the smell.

Television Set: Highly-addictive piece of furniture that plays a lot of old movies, which makes a lot of dead people look at least as alive as you and me.

Terminal: Where you get off; not necessarily at the end of the line.

Terrorism, Economic: Havoc wreaked in North Carolina by putting people out of work temporarily (lost job) or permanently (lost life).

"Thanks for the Memories:" Theme song sung by world-famous entertainer Bob Hope (*which see*) to his favorite audiences and by every smoker to his favorite brand.

Thinwalking: Type of walking done to get yourself thin; specifically: walking as fast as you comfortably can for as long as you comfortably can.

Thigh Muscles: Dicey things to suddenly rely on in a pinch, if you haven't been relying on them for much of anything the last decade or three.

Third Army: Fairly large collection of fatigue-clad guys and gals, easily concealed behind the "screen" a smoker generates each morning between shower and shave.

Three Mile Island: Nuclear reactor in Pennsylvania that hiccupped back in the late 1970's; of all God's creations, nuclear reactors are perhaps the last ones we'd like to see hiccup.

Three Months: Average amount of time needed to undo about three decades of lung damage caused by smoking; also: time period that's approximately three months longer than lifelong smokers **think** it should take.

Titration: Adding one chemical to a different chemical till they exactly balance each other out chemically, which you determine by observing the changes in a "marker" (usually another chemical).

Toast: The raising and touching of glasses, to celebrate something good that has happened or that you'd like to see happen; frequent occurrence at big oil companies and big tobacco companies (*which see*).

Tobacco Company Executives: Historically: Fascinating individuals indirectly responsible for tearing cities apart (see also: **Civil Engineers**).

Tooth Fairy: Small creature who children believe replaces their under-pillow baby teeth with cash money while they're asleep; also: the only hope smoker has of getting his battered lung tissue replaced if he never stops lighting up.

Toothpick: Cigarette-shaped piece of sharp-pointed wood, far less likely to kill you than a lot of other cigarette-shaped things you stick in your mouth.

Toxic Waste: What the rest of society can't seem to get rid of and what smokers can't seem to get enough of.

Transplants: Transferring organs — heart, lungs, liver, etc. — from one person to another; necessary to correct defects of birth or defects from a half-century of abuse; often effective for as long as a month or two.

Tummy Churning: Physiological condition, rarely fatal, that your Subconscious Mind lays on you when you try to give up **any** abusive substance.

Twelve Years Old: To Little League Coach: ideal age to start hitting a curveball; To Philip Morris: ideal age to start lighting a Marlboro.

Two Million Dollars a Year: Average 1991 salary of baseball superstars; what whole **teams** used to be paid, till the landmark discovery on the part of the Players Union that team owners weren't losing as much on every three dollars-for-seven ounces cup of beer as was originally thought.

Umpire: Referee in baseball; usually not in the same physical condition as the people who are **playing** the game — sometimes embarrassingly so.

Undertaker: Rather artless juxtaposition of words, when you get right down to it.

Unicorn: Mythical, horselike creature with single horn growing out of its head; always depicted as gentle or playful and why not, since no one's ever had one over for dinner.

Universe: To astronomers: "Everything 'out there.'"
          To you: "Everything 'in here.'"

Valium: Son of Librium (*which see*).

Vesuvius: Volcano in Italy that blew up bigtime in 79 A. D. and has hiccupped once or twice since then.

Vomit: Forceful regurgitation of stomach contents; also: what anti-smoking activists make smokers want to do.

Waffle: Technically: Item of breakfast food with lots of "holes" in it, so easily folded. Slang: What happens when our backbones turn to breakfast food.

Walk Yourself Thin Program: A way of getting thin without going on a diet; derived from very funny, very clever book written by...guess who?

Walking (brisk): Best way to find out how little of your physical ability you've lost to smoking (see also: **National Debt, the**).

Walls: Usually fairly-sturdy structures, purposely put in the way of alcoholics to make driving a car an even **greater** challenge (see also: **Small Children**); also: things that suddenly seem inviting to climb, when you're withdrawing from an addictive substance.

Water Skiing: The way a lot of fat people have decided is the best way to take off weight, since all you need is a boat and a driver and a pair of skis and a line and a body of water and a nice day and......

Weakling: People who spend a great deal of time telling you why they don't have time to do something.

Weed: What a Marlboro was, before it became your best friend.

Weight Gain: Moderate but temporary addition to body weight when you quit smoking; also: large and permanent addition to body weight if you don't (see: **Coffin**).

Western World: Just west of the Eastern World; includes United States and Europe I think.

Wild Horses: Pack of animals that, once in motion, are hard to stop; thus: what it should take to get you smoking again once you've quit — though not if Philip Morris's advertising agency has anything to say about it.

Wimps: First cousins of geeks (*which see*).

Windfall Profits: What people spend half their time trying to make and the other half resenting everyone who does.

Winston: Diamond merchant from New York (b. "Weinstein); death merchant from North Carolina (b. "harmless vice").

Worldly: A certain panache (*which see*) that you get by traveling to a lot of foreign countries or by lighting a cigarette on your front porch.

Yeltsin, Boris N. (b. 1931): Charismatic President of Russia who defied 1991 coup that toppled Gorbachev (*which see*), brought that one back to life, only to form more powerful government while Soviet President was gone.

Zero: The average number of people who will notice you've quite smoking after you do; therefore: the total number of people you were **impressing** with your habit before you did.

Zillionaire: Richer than lots and lots of people (see: **Reynolds, R. J.; Lorillard, P.; etc.**).

Zip Code: Postal zone, within which all addresses have the same five-number code; as far away as a non-smoker would like to stay from his smoking kinfolk.

Index

A

M

N

When you **really have**…

…just let us know and we'll send you this beautiful sticker, so you can let **other smokers** know you have!

Why?

So maybe they can, too!

Why else?

To remind **yourself**, every time you get behind the wheel, of what you've accomplished -- and to remind yourself to **keep** accomplishing it, every day of your new life!

Simply send us a Xerox of this page with the bottom all filled out, along with your **PROOF OF PURCHASE**, and we'll send you your sticker by return mail.

Moon River Publishing • P. O. Box 5244 • Ventura, CA 93005

Yes, David, I **really have**! So please send me my free (check one)
- ❏ Bumper sticker
- ❏ Window sticker

—so I can let the **World** know I have!

Enclosed is my **REGISTER RECEIPT** or other **PROOF OF PURCHASE** for *Dying for a Smoke*.

Name_____

Address:_____

City/State/Zip:_____

Phone No.: (_____)_____ _____

Enjoy the Book? Then You'll FLIP over the Audiocassette Program!

DYING FOR A SMOKE

David A. Rives
Author of *Walk Yourself Thin*

If you can stop smoking with the book alone, FANTASTIC!! But, if you'd like to **listen** to a few tips as well, the *Dying for a Smoke* Audiocassette Program is made for you!

Like to become an even BIGGER Winner?! This can help!

"...brilliant!"

"...delightful!"

"...one of the funniest books I've ever read — and one of the most highly-motivating!"

"...you saved my life!"

Available wherever books are sold; or call

1-800-THINWALK

(1-800-64-TAPES in Canada)

for location nearest you.

Or simply use the handy ordering form on the previous page!

You Can't Lose!

Dear Smoker:

Really can't quit?

Angry that you spent **20 bucks** on a **book** and not on the carton of cigarettes you were **going** to buy?!

No problem: Just send **us** the book, along with proof of purchase, and **we'll** buy you the cigarettes!

Fair enough?

(P. S. Send everything "Book Rate.")

Moon River Publishing • P. O. Box 5244 • Ventura, CA 93005
Dear David:

After reading *Dying for a Smoke* at least once, I've decided that life without cigarettes is just too terrifying to even consider. As a result, I have decided to take advantage of your **"You Can't Lose"** offer and am sending you:

- My copy of the **book**
- The **register receipt** (or other **proof-of-purchase**) for the book*
- A **Xerox of this page**, all filled out.

Please send a carton of my favorite brand of cigarettes**—

_____

—to the following:

Name_____

Address:_____

City/State/Zip:_____

Phone No.: (___)_____

Sorry it didn't work out!

However, I **would** like to order the things I've indicated **two pages back!**

*Books not accompanied by proof of purchase will simply be given to the D. A. R. E. Program.
**Moon River reserves the right to supply other-than-carton quantities of cigarettes outside the continental United States, though the value of the cigarettes supplied will always be of approximately equal value to the retail price of *Dying for a Smoke*.